# Negotiating the Social Borderlands

Portraits of Young People with Disabilities
and
Their Struggles for Positive Relationships

Janet Sauer

Published by American Association on Intellectual and Developmental Disabilities (AAIDD)
501 Third Street, NW
Suite 200
Washington, DC 20001–2760

**Library of Congress Cataloging-in-Publication Data**

Sauer, Janet Story.
  Negotiating the social borderlands : portraits of young people with significant disabilities and their struggle for positive relationships / Janet Story Sauer.
     p. cm.
  1. Developmentally disabled youth—Case studies. 2. Interpersonal relations—Case studies. 3. Interpersonal communication—Case studies. 4. Social interaction in youth—Case studies. I. American Association on Intellectual and Developmental Disabilities. II. Title.
  HV1570.S28 2012
  155.45'2—dc23
                        2012036724

# Contents

*I dedicate this book to my family, the participants,*
*and all who communicate and live in unconventional ways.*

# Introduction

The purpose of this book is to provide readers with portrait narratives of the lives of three young people with significant disabilities. These portraits illustrate the complexities involved in capturing their stories. Early in my teacher education, I learned about the Americans with Disabilities Act of 1990, which recognizes disability as "a natural part of the human experience" and ensures children's rights to "contribute to society, and experience full integration and inclusion into all aspects of society." I did not fully appreciate the meaning behind these words until I began to understand my role in contributing to the disability experience as a community service provider, a teacher, a mother, and a citizen.

In writing this book, I chose portraiture to narrate the stories of these young people and to capture what Harvard researcher Sara Lawrence-Lightfoot (1983) referred to as the "myriad dimensions" of each person. Portraiture requires a balance between empirical description and aesthetic expression (Lawrence-Lightfoot & Davis, 1997). The form, which provides a unique opportunity to capture the nuances and complexities of life, is best known for capturing social contexts in general, as in Lawrence-Lightfoot's (1983) *The Good High School*. It has only recently been used to study students with disabilities considered "mild" (Connor, 2006; McNeil, 2005) or students with other minority statuses, such as race, class, or gender (Chapman, 2007). To my knowledge, this is the first set of portrait narratives focusing on the lives of young people considered to have significant disabilities.

This book is written for a broad audience. First, for university students in education, counseling, sociology, nursing, criminal justice, or other fields where one would expect to interact directly with people with disabilities and their families, this book offers a naturally complex and sensitive portrayal of three personal stories in which a variety of contextualized issues can be examined and discussed in light of readers' own practices and policies. Second, parents, policy designers, and the community at large will potentially find this book helpful in developing a greater understanding of the ways in which people might inadvertently contribute to the continued stigmatizing attitudes and behaviors toward people with impairments. It is generally understood that to effect

1

change, we must first exercise self-awareness and through our daily interactions we can begin to change ourselves.

My career has provided me with experiences in a wide range of contexts, across geographies both physical and social. After college I co-taught an urban integration video course to high school students in Boston, and later as a Peace Corps volunteer, I videotaped teachers in the Breakthrough to Literacy program for young children in Botswana, Africa. In one small rural village, I first noticed how an imaginative teacher creatively adapted the local classroom so one of her students who had cerebral palsy could naturally participate in the learning alongside his classmates.

Upon returning to the United States, I joined a fully bilingual school on the Navajo Reservation. During an afternoon high school class where the students enacted and videotaped their authored scripts, I realized that one of my students could not read. For months I had been negotiating cultural and linguistic differences among myself and my students, their families, and the wider community. Like I had in Botswana, I was preoccupied with addressing the more obvious need to learn the language and social customs of interaction, so I had not readily noticed a student's learning difference. I had not yet learned to pay close attention, to observe and reflect. However, this realization instigated a need for action, and I began both my personal and professional journey into studying the experiences of people with disabilities. It was several years later before I was able to value their stories not just as a teacher who came to understand how much I could learn from people with disabilities but as a mother whose first child was born with an extra chromosome. Although my child's experiences are not the focus of this book, my emerging skills as a teacher researcher undoubtedly interacted with my evolving role as a young mother.

It was during my doctoral program that I was given an assignment to practice audio-recording, transcribing, and analyzing a short situation. I recorded my family's dinner-time conversation. Upon listening to the scene again and again, a pattern of communication emerged whereby my eldest son was continually interrupted by me, my husband, and our younger son. I was a practicing elementary special education teacher when our first son was born and diagnosed with trisomy 21. For nearly all of his 8 years of life, he had been provided with speech-language therapy, and my husband and I had become well versed in the practices and expectations of the therapists and special educators. We knew the importance of encouraging him to talk, the positive effect of wait time and active listening. In fact, we thought we were following the prescribed recommendations of the field, until I analyzed the transcriptions.

The data suggested otherwise, that our daily interactions actually discouraged rather than supported our son's verbal self-expression. Upon listening to the audio and rereading the transcripts, I felt for the first time what it might be like to be someone with so much to say but rarely given the opportunity to share my thoughts, to ask questions, to negotiate relationships, and to develop shared understanding. The event left me wondering about other young people with communication impairments and how they experience social interactions. I wanted to learn from young people with unconventional communication how and with whom they developed *local understanding*, "an educational dialogic grounded in reciprocal instructional relationships among individuals with and without disabilities" (Kliewer & Biklen, 2007, p. 2580), where people with significant disabilities are viewed as full-fledged members. Children with significant disabilities are often determined to be communicatively incompetent when their behavior is judged against a set of norms by adults unfamiliar to the children or by those who have not been able to find ways of sharing meaning with the children. Researchers focusing on student interactions and linguists caution against making assumptions about students who might not readily engage in interactions (Cazden, 2001; Hymes, 1973).

Taking into account this idea, I decided to use qualitative techniques of inquiry to examine the complexities involved in the co-construction of meaning between three young people with significant disabilities and their communication partners. I wanted to know how deep relationships developed between one person with a significant disability and another person where the *disability* construct was not the focus. The purpose of the study, on which this book is based, was to describe (a) the contexts where positive reciprocal relationships developed between young people with significant disabilities and nondisabled people and (b) how these relationships developed from the perspectives of the various players.

An inquiry into the social worlds of young people with communication disabilities, a particularly vulnerable minority (Broer, Doyle, & Giangreco, 2005; Holmes, 1998; Lewis & Kellet, 2005; Lloyd-Smith & Tarr, 2000; Tassé, Schalock, Thompson, & Wehmeyer, 2005), calls the qualitative researcher to find a way to capture and relay their stories in a sensitive and respectful manner. I believe that using terminology such as "case studies" to report my findings would serve only to perpetuate the clinical and dehumanizing orientation of people labeled with disabilities and that it does not contribute to the recognition of children's perspectives as valuable resources. McDermott (1993) emphasizes the power of language when he writes, "Language is not a neutral medium; it comes to us loaded with social structure" (p. 293). It is with this understanding of the power of language that I sought another way to convey what I observed and experienced during this study. As I describe in the first chapter in greater depth, I decided to use a portraiture research methodology to document the lived experiences of my three primary participants: David, age 10 and diagnosed with autism; Katie, age 17 and diagnosed with Down syndrome; and Marie, age 8 and diagnosed with Rett syndrome.[1]

"One of the primary characteristics of contemporary, postmodern qualitative research," writes Pugach (2001), "is the commitment to bring to the surface stories of those whose voices have not been heard" (p. 443). To acknowledge the three young

---

[1] All names are pseudonyms.

people labeled with significant disabilities whose daily lives as contributing members of society I studied for nearly a year, I made an effort to give them opportunities to share their perspectives more directly. For instance, I examined their drawings and writings, which are interspersed throughout the following portraits. I also gave them digital audio recorders for weeks at a time. In some circumstances, the young people spoke or sang directly into the recorder; other times their family members recorded interactions or simply used the recorder in ways similar to a journal to describe their relationship with their sibling or daughter or son. Katie, the eldest of the three, ended up taking the recorder everywhere she went and recorded hundreds of hours of audio, occasionally interviewing people with whom she typically interacted. In fact, her use of the recorder at times got her into social situations her parents thought were troublesome. These qualitative research techniques, along with more traditional approaches including my role as participant observer (Bogdan & Biklen, 2003), were used in an effort to answer the question "What are the perspectives about their relationships of the children and young people considered to have disabilities?"

There are several challenges to identify and document the perspectives and experiences of young people with significant disabilities. To spend the time necessary to become familiar with the nuances of their communication as well as earn their trust and that of their families, I decided to limit myself to three primary participants. William Ayers (1989) suggests in his analysis of early childhood teachers' portraits that one can "discover a lot about a few teachers rather than a little about a lot of teachers" (p. 4). He explains that there is value in examining the particular, especially when linking portraits to one another and to the broader "cultural and institutional context" (p. 126).

Overall, I found the relationships I observed and eventually participated in to be less than straightforward. Each young person's relationships differed in their own complexities, and yet, when read together, a broad theme emerged where all three young persons struggled with social borders reflecting historical segregation based on misunderstanding. In her often-cited book about the history of the Chicano people, Anzaldua (1999) describes the presence of borderlands "whenever two or more cultures edge each other ... where the space between two individuals shrinks with intimacy." I incorporate this idea in the title of the book to illustrate what many describe as a different culture, those contexts where people with disabilities live, as though they are different from some other presumed "normal world."

As teachers, therapists, or social workers, we are often discouraged from getting to know our students or clients in personal ways. Except when the children are very young and our professions require us to visit them in their homes, we rarely if ever engage with these young people in their homes and neighborhoods. Often our schedules and "caseloads" restrict us from the opportunities to interact with the children across contexts. Therefore, we begin to become acculturated in habits of interaction where we might forget to see the children as fully human, as "one of us." Our professions expound the value of developing positive relationships with the families of our students and clients, yet social customs and discourse seem to build borders between us.

Lawrence-Lightfoot (2003) takes up Anzaldua's idea of borderlands in her description of some parent and teacher relationships: "Negotiating family-school borders is, at best, an imperfect and delicate enterprise" (p. 228). The professionals in the portraits I narrate in this book similarly provide a range of responses that seem to reflect our society in general. Although I sought positive examples for the rest of us to learn from, I found some interactions disheartening, especially in my professional role as a teacher educator. That said, I think it is important to acknowledge what is happening, and I hope we will learn from a variety of examples.

The conclusions that I draw here are my own and reflect my cultural biases and personal experiences. However, when reading these three portraits of young people with significant disabilities, I expect some readers will readily find examples of routines and discourse common to many American public schools and therapeutic contexts. It is my hope that readers might come to see themselves in these scenes and recognize patterns of interaction in their own lives where they notice stigmatizing social routines and challenge them in order to engage in meaningful reciprocal relationships with people with disabilities.

It is especially noteworthy that many of the professionals (as well as the family members) described in this book examined my field notes and transcriptions and engaged in reflective thinking alongside me. We found that in many successful reciprocal relationships, each member seemed to embark on elements of risk taking in an effort to challenge those borders. In fact, one of the most powerful findings was the documented efforts of the young people themselves to break free of these routines. Their sense of agency offers readers inspiration, if we are wise enough and listen carefully enough to what they have to say regardless of the manner in which they might communicate.

Each of the three portraits is organized into four parts. The first section introduces the young person broadly on the basis of what I found to be a situation that exemplified one of the themes or captured their personality. The second section describes the various social contexts in which the young person most often spent his or her time. In the third section, I illustrate the different ways in which individuals in David's, Katie's, and Marie's lives developed relationships. The fourth section of each portrait provides an analysis of the themes that emerged and some probing questions that address implications for practitioners. Although the broad theme of negotiating and contesting the social borders emerged in each portrait, there were variations and other themes that emerged among the different primary participants, which I discuss in the final chapter.

# Chapter I

# Portraiture as a Portal into Local Understanding

Portraiture is a form of qualitative inquiry that provides a portal into local understanding (Kliewer & Biklen, 2007). Using Geertz's (1983) anthropological perspective that values local knowledge, Kliewer and Biklen (2007) describe local understanding as "the recognition of an individual's citizenship and the crafting of responsive contexts" (p. 2581). Practitioners in the field of special education and therapeutic and support services for our youth with significant disabilities are often criticized by those intended to be served in these systems as insensitive, unable, or unwilling to actively listen and engage in equitable collaboration. By contrast, practitioners who seem to understand that cultural meanings are negotiated may recognize that systems that might typically stigmatize or dehumanize marginalized groups, such as our youth with significant disabilities, can be reconstituted in ways that acknowledge and ascribe value to them. In other words, our communities, schools, and homes are possible sites of local understanding, where positive, reciprocal relationships offer opportunities for us to re-create systems that are too often experienced as dehumanizing or oppressive.

My search for local understanding in the lives of young people with disabilities is here illustrated through Lawrence-Lightfoot's *portraiture,* as a way to "create a narrative that . . . convey[s] the authority, wisdom, and perspective of the 'subjects'" who might see themselves in the narrative as "fully attended to, recognized, appreciated, respected, and scrutinized" (2005, p. 6). I began by sharing a one-page study description with families through a community-based family support group located in an upper Midwestern mid-sized city. I made home visits with the handful of families who responded, during which I explained the study in greater detail and offered information about confidentiality and consent. I was interested in recruiting families who lived in different school districts as

I hoped to explore these differences and their possible impact. However, I was somewhat restricted by the distance—two of the families lived nearly 60 miles apart—as I planned to spend extensive amounts of time with each family over an academic year. In the end, using purposeful and snowball samples of convenience, I selected three families (Bogdan & Biklen, 2003; Maxwell, 1992). These three families and their extended support personnel shared their daily lives, offering a sort of portal into local understanding so that others may learn from their experiences. By moving "closer to the unique characteristics of a person," writes Lawrence-Lightfoot (2005), we might discover the universal.

## METHOD AND PROCEDURES

Data collection included a variety of forms: detailed field notes as a participant observer, transcripts from audiotaped open-ended interviews and conversations with the participants, and artifacts. Artifacts included official educational records, informal communication via letters, postcards, and e-mail, and students' work. The field notes reflected detailed descriptions of the physical environments and behaviors I observed. The field notes included a record of my own behaviors, decisions, and reflections as well because I was a participant observer throughout this study (Bogdan & Biklen, 2003; Brantlinger, Goode, 1994; Kasa-Hendrickson & Broderick, 2009; Klein, & Guskin, 1994; Linneman, 2001).

Although my visits with each of the primary participants differed somewhat, typically I made arrangements with the young person's mother through phone calls or e-mails a week prior to the visit. I never asked the parents to bring their child to me or to another location outside the home or school; instead I asked for permission to join them or their child in an activity where they were already scheduled. Occasionally I consented to the parents' (or child's) request to take their child to the park, the library, or for a bike ride.

The data I collected were descriptive, which is another feature of qualitative study designs (Bogdan & Biklen, 2003). I always carried a pocket-sized notebook with me in which I sketched maps and noted quotes during my visits, but sometimes, when I joined the participants on the swings or in the swimming pool, I would sit in my car immediately after visits filling pages with more information about what I saw, heard, and thought about. Eventually, I took to recording my comments and thoughts on my voice recorder because it allowed me a much faster way to record notes than in written form. Later, I typed up my handwritten and recorded notes into more formal field notes that included summary statements in memo form.

My initial sets of field notes included many drawings and descriptions of the physical settings and people, along with reflective statements and questions. However, after I developed rapport with each family, generally after the first couple of visits, I asked for and received permission to record the conversations and incidental sounds during my visits. As a consequence, my subsequent field notes became far more detailed, totaling nearly 1,000 pages at the completion of the study.

Furthermore, I assembled contact logs for each primary participant and his or her secondary participants. These provided me with an overview of the contact dates, times, content, and methodology. The combined logs at the end of the study filled nearly 12 pages. The logs provided me with easy retrieval information for specific transcripts or audio files that I wanted to see or listen to again at a later time. This became helpful for data analysis, which I conducted throughout the study using constant-comparative procedures (Bogdan & Biklen, 2003; Glaser, 1978).

I also used Gee's (1999) discourse analysis based on what I noticed were patterns of communication during the naturally occurring interactions. Brantlinger, Jimenez, Klingner, Pugach, and Richardson (2005) describe discourse analysis as the study of "interactional situations, structures of talk, and communicative exchanges" (p. 197), whereas Bogdan and Biklen (2003) explain discourse as a way of understanding relationships. Gee (1999) offers the idea of including nonverbal communicative acts, such as body, space, and timing within interactions. He emphasizes the value of reflective time, noting, "The small child whom the teacher assumed made no sense at sharing time looks a lot smarter after a little reflection" (Gee, 2005, p. xi). Therefore, on reviewing my data repeatedly and reflecting over time, I noted recurring comments or behaviors within and across participants, hunches, and questions to ask the participants in successive conversations. Subsequently, I developed an initial coding scheme that I then narrowed over time after additional field work, reviewing the data, and consulting with the participants and other scholars in literacy and qualitative methodology. These codes were then organized into themes with the supporting data vignettes, artifacts, and quotes that illustrated them.

## CONTEXTUALIZING THE PORTRAITS

David, Katie, and Marie all lived within an 80-mile radius of each other in their family homes. Both David's and Katie's parents relocated to the area after having children, but all are native Midwesterners and ethnically Caucasian Anglo-Saxon descendants. Although Katie was born in the southwestern part of the United States, shortly after learning she had trisomy 21, her mother explained, they had moved back to the upper Midwest to be closer to family, "so that we could all get to know and support each other."

Katie's hometown was first settled by the French fur traders who moved their goods up and down the Mississippi River. The traders and their Northern European compatriots named the town Hutton (the name of the town has been changed). One remnant of Hutton's early prosperity is the large Victorian-style wood and quarried limestone homes built on the river bluffs. As the town began to expand, engineers found ways to circumvent the steep cliffs, building homes on the sides and atop the bluffs. Katie and her family live in one of these homes, in the historic heart of Hutton.

David and his family live atop the bluffs in a ranch-styled home, about 30 miles from the small city of Hutton. After the Industrial Revolution, Hutton's industry changed from trade to meat packing in large red brick factories. Many of Hutton's residents worked in the factories packaging the beef, poultry, and pork that were raised on the family farms just beyond the bluffs.

Marie's father grew up on a family farm, about 40 miles from Hutton, but he settled with his family in a nearby small town called Verstanburg. Both Marie and David traveled from their respective towns to Hutton for therapy services, so although their lives were different in many ways, all three of my primary participants spent some of their time every week in Hutton.

One lifetime Hutton resident told me, "A lot of people stay here, and many are afraid of stretching, so we have limited exposure to the rest of America. We're sort of a micro-community of America." He explained, "We have labor roots and most of us are blue-collar workers with traditional values." He added, with some hesitation, "We're unaccepting of differences." His comments illustrate the tension I frequently observed among people who interacted with David, Katie, and Marie and the challenges they met as they tried to negotiate shared positive relationships.

CHAPTER 2

# David's Portrait

FIGURE 1. *David's Self Portrait*

FIGURE 2. *David's mother's drawing of him.*

**MEETING DAVID: "HE IS BEAUTIFUL."**

It was an early summer day. I had been driving for over an hour, along mostly winding country roads. I passed through only one town with any traffic lights on my drive to David's house in the town of Hutton. I was anxious with the uncertainty of not knowing just what to expect upon meeting David and his family. David's mother, Robin, and I had e-mailed and phoned each other for nearly a year, but we had not met. In one of those exchanges, I asked Robin for permission to show David's photograph in a presentation. On giving me her consent, she wrote: "I don't have a problem with you using his picture. He is beautiful." While driving along the river road, I remembered David's picture, his fair tanned skin, brown eyes, and silky thin light brown hair. My knowledge about David was limited to his photograph, a diagnosis of autism, and his mother's comments. "David communicates with behavior; that's what he does," she said. The night before that first visit to their house, Robin told me he had bitten her and they were "working with him on keeping his clothes on." She added, "If it turns out that we're not right, if we're not a good match, just let us know." This comment echoed in my mind throughout the following months. I wondered whether she meant that David did not have positive reciprocal relationships (the topic of my study) or whether she anticipated that I might abandon them like so many others in the special service system seemed to do.

I pulled into the gravel driveway and parked my station wagon between their four-door Buick and their new camper. I walked up the steps of the bi-level limestone and wood house and knocked on the screen door. "C'mon in!" A 12-year-old girl opened the door, her Swiss heritage revealing itself in her broad shoulders, blonde hair, and high rosy cheeks. "I'm Anastasia and this is David," she said stepping back and to the side of her brother, who sat immediately inside the door on the floor laying out playing cards in front of him. "Hi, David," I said. He looked up briefly at me and then leaned over his cards, as though he was shielding them from me. David was barefooted and wearing a t-shirt and a pair of boxer shorts patterned with animal drawings. He looked much like I remembered him from his picture except that his skin looked even fairer. He was, as his mother had said, beautiful.

I was quickly swept up into introductions and then conversations with the rest of the family, and I did not interact directly again with David until later during that initial visit, when we looked through the family picture album. But first, as was often the case in David's home, I was offered to join the family in a homemade snack. David's sister Anastasia and their 6-year-old brother, Bobby, had been at swimming lessons earlier in the morning and they eagerly ate Robin's freshly baked poppy seed muffins. I sat at the round kitchen table talking with Robin and her husband, Dan, who, like Robin, was a teacher and thus able to be home for the summer with the children. When I told the family that I would be using pseudonyms in my field notes, David's younger brother was excited, and he offered the name of a favorite dinosaur character from one of his books: Bob. So, Bobby, Anastasia, and David sat alongside each other eating muffins while I explained to them and their parents that the purpose of my study was to understand David's communication and relationships.

Upon finishing her muffin, Anastasia asked her mother, "Can I go get the photo album and share it?" "He *loves* pictures," Robin said, referring to David. Thus began a litany of descriptions about David by his family that morning while I sat with them in their kitchen:

David is really good at puzzles. He can do it when the pieces are upside down. He's always been very good at shapes. David is a reader. Ever since he was little he would pick out books at the library. David likes to get on the computer and change the pictures on the screen. He gets into files and moves things around. You like pretzels, don't you, David? Yeah, one time after all the pretzels were gone, he licked all the salt. Yeah, he loves salt.

David's family was quick to describe David in positive ways that revealed their affinity for him. They also shared their uncertainty about their interpretations of his communication and how this seemed to make them, particularly his mother, feel inadequate.

He doesn't like crunchy food. David would probably like to swim if he could without any clothes on. He doesn't like to keep his clothes on. I don't know why. Maybe they itch him. Or maybe he's hot. Or, the other day, after he took off his clothes, he pooped, so it may be sometimes that he has to go to the bathroom. We use some sign and PECS.[1] We need to do more.

Nearly a year after this conversation, Robin continued to say things like, "We need to do more," but what "more" meant was continually debated. Also, other idiosyncratic or peculiar behaviors might have been considered acceptable, but David's aversion to keeping his clothes on went beyond "appropriate" behavior and led people to question his membership in social contexts.

The information I gleaned during that lengthy discussion, though helpful regarding David's interests and a clear indication that his family acknowledged him as an individual, did little to help me understand David's storyline, his way of being in the world. I wanted to find out from him directly more about how he experienced life. David did not verbally talk to me about himself that day or on any subsequent visit during my study, but I soon entered into my own relationship with him. The following interaction shows the beginning of that relationship. Anastasia was turning the pages in the photo album. Bobby got up from his chair and stood behind his sister, looking over her shoulder at the pictures. After eating his muffin, David returned to his cards on the floor, where he sat cross-legged. I sat to one side of Anastasia, who was pointing to a picture of a toddler whose face was covered in pudding. It was David. "When *I* was little, *I* used to paint my arms purple," she said looking up and over at her mother, but I sensed she was talking to me, assuring me that it was perfectly normal for little children to mess themselves up with food. It was as though she wanted to make sure I would not view David as deviant.

I do not know what then prompted David to get up, dropping his cards to the floor, and join us at the table. Perhaps he had grown bored with the cards. Perhaps he just

---

[1] Robin is referring to a visual method of communication, where pictures (or black-line drawings) are used in the exchange of thoughts in place of or in addition to verbal speech. PECS stands for Picture Exchange Communication System.

noticed the photo album and he wanted to look at the pictures. Or maybe he had been listening to us talk about him and wanted to assert himself and be part of the conversation. Whatever the reason, he quickly moved in between me and Anastasia, slightly pushing his sister so she would move to the now empty chair on her other side. "Move over, sister," Robin said, in what I learned was her way of giving David a voice. Robin and others who knew David well often voiced their interpretations of David's communication-through-action like this, and I saw it as a meaningful way to empower him. Then Robin turned to me and said, "He's going to want to start at the beginning," at which point David closed the album and began looking at the pictures on the first page.

Although David took control of turning the pages of the photo album, Anastasia continued to provide the running commentary, thus maintaining her control of the conversation. In this way, people's voices might have disempowered David. "That's you, David!" David paused in response, looking carefully at the pictures, and then he sort of hopped up in his chair, in what seemed to indicate his happiness. Moments later, David pointed to a different photograph, and Robin leaned over to see what he was pointing to. "David," she said loudly and a bit more slowly than one would conventionally converse. "That's David," she said again to her son. I noticed Robin had begun speaking to David in the third person. Then I put my finger beside his on the picture and asked him, "Is that you, David?" He did not look up at me or make a sound but neither did he shirk away when our hands touched; instead we both left our hands touching for an unusually long time before the family resumed the conversation and David returned to turning the pages of the album.

## DAVID'S SOCIAL WORLDS: SHRINKING SOCIAL BORDERS

*Social and Clinical Services: Doin' David and the Search for a Treatment*

Unlike other 10-year-olds, who might spend much of their time playing with their age-mates, David spent much of his time among adults: those paid to work on changing his behaviors. Consequently, David's opportunities for developing relationships with typical peers or with other people outside specialized service systems were seriously limited. In the search for "an answer" or treatment for his differences, David was increasingly constrained to hospital-like environments where experts made countless assessments and prescribed lists of special therapies and materials. The relationships between David and the social and clinical staff were unequal and unstable, but occasionally some people managed to develop a shared understanding with him, where he was then viewed more as a person with thoughts and feelings similar to their own.

Despite the fact that many of these adults described David as "intelligent" and "quick to learn," his time was primarily taken up with specialized services that did not appear to support the idea of smartness, nor did these offer him activities that seemed very intrinsically motivating. Twice a week in the evenings, David and his mother or father traveled 30 minutes each way to therapy sessions in Hutton. "It's better now," Robin explained, "We used to have to drive further." There David saw three therapists: a speech-language pathologist (SLP), an occupational therapist (OT), and a physical therapist (PT). It is worth noting that the therapists made a great effort to make the hallway and therapy rooms colorful and visually attractive to children, with paintings of fish and decorations hanging from the ceilings. They also designed the new building to include a kitchen, much like one would find in a middle-class house. Yet David usually spent most of his hour-and-a-half-long sessions assembling puzzles, riding a scooter or swinging, and producing speech sounds, sign language, and pictures on command for the therapists. The only time I saw a child without disabilities there was in the waiting room of the building, and the child was a sibling of a child with a disability. Therefore, David had no opportunities for interactions with other children during the therapy sessions.

David's SLP was working with him on making use of various forms of communication. While sitting in the therapists' waiting room one day with Robin and all three of her children, the SLP told me, "We're pushing the Dynavox." (The Dynavox is a book-sized speech-generating device.) The SLP and OT asked Robin whether she had charged the batteries for the Dynavox and whether she could create a transition page of pictures to add to it. Robin said she had but that soon she would have to replace the battery, indicating frustration with its expense. Another time they conferred about the Dynavox, Robin said, "I like 'help me' a lot. And 'I'm finished.'" They discussed the benefits between the statements "no" and "I need a break" and decided Robin would change "no" to "I need a break." "We modeled 'I need a break' using the switch the other day," the therapist said. She explained how she hit the switch and got a break, which meant lying down on a large blue mat and getting squished by another therapist. "Whoa, he went right over to it [the switch]," she recalled with surprised enthusiasm. David's OT added with similar surprise that she had provided David with a number of wooden shapes,[2] and when she told him "Make an 'A,'" he did. Apparently, she asked David to assemble many different letters of the alphabet, and he quickly responded with the correct answer each time.

In addition to weekly therapy sessions, David took several day trips (80 miles each way) and had weeklong intensive sessions at a university research hospital. I joined him, his parents, and his special education teacher on one of these trips. The rooms were located on an upper floor of a huge multibuilding research hospital complex, and their long halls and white-colored observation rooms resembled those of hospitals. The one area in which David found something of interest was in the waiting room where they

---

[2] The shapes the OT laid on a table for David were taken from a writing curriculum called "Handwriting Without Tears." The wooden pieces consist of a collection of straight and curved pieces that can easily be used to construct alphabetic letters.

had a large, enclosed three-dimensional puzzle. But the puzzle was not designed to be very interactive, and so the children who shared David's interest sat beside each other in chairs just watching it. "I hope they can give us an answer," the teacher said. Next, several therapists specializing in autism asked David's parents questions and gave them advice while they observed David. The therapists gave David's parents a social story about not taking clothes off. [3] They also discussed the idea of allowing David a time and place where he could stay naked. Robin and Dan decided that David could be without his clothes in either the upstairs bathroom or in his bedroom. In case David was taking his clothing off because he was bothered by their texture, his parents purchased various pairs of pants of different fabrics and cut out all the tags. But David seemed to prefer loose-fitting boxer shorts and he had a favorite t-shirt, which Robin washed daily (and she also handmade clothes for him). One day Robin casually speculated that David's "disrobing" might have been "his way to protest," but I did not hear any further discussion of this idea.

For several years, David had been using "Therapeutic Listening"[4] CDs for at least 30 minutes a day and swinging in the basement on a hammock; both of these activities were considered to be methods for helping David integrate sensory input, something the specialists thought might be related to David's "behaviors." One therapist suggested that David get a tunnel to climb through and a "body sock," which the family immediately did and which David regularly sought both at home and at school. (Other students and David's family members sometimes accompanied him in the tunnel and the body sock.) The hospital specialists discussed adding more pictures to David's Dynavox. They also suggested that the family provide David with "more structure" during summer and regular "deep tissue massage" to help David regulate sensory input.

Though David's parents and teacher seemed optimistic upon leaving the hospital, there were several problems with trying to implement all the specialized therapies and support systems. First, there were so many different professionals with different recommendations that it was difficult for the family to follow through with all of them and

---

[3] Social stories are a trademarked name for a tool designed by Carol Gray in 1991 to assist children with autism in understanding social situations. According to the Web site for the Gray Center for Social Learning and Understanding, "A Social Story™ describes a situation, skill, or concept in terms of relevant social cues, perspectives, and common responses in a specifically defined style and format. The goal of a Social Story™ is to share accurate social information in a patient and reassuring manner that is easily understood by its audience. Half of all Social Stories™ developed should affirm something that an individual does well. Although the goal of a Story™ should never be to change the individual's behavior, that individual's improved understanding of events and expectations may lead to more effective responses." See http://www.thegraycenter.org/socialstorywhat.cfm for additional information.

[4] Therapeutic Listening is a trademarked program occupational therapists use to assist people who have difficulty integrating their senses. Studies where Therapeutic Listening is used refer to it as an intervention. For an example, see the March–April 2007 issue of the *American Journal of Occupational Therapy*, where Leah Hall (MS, OTR/L) and Jane Case-Smith (EdD, OTR/L, FAOTA) used Therapeutic Listening with children diagnosed with sensory processing disorders and visual-motor delays.

to coordinate their implementation with the other service providers. Second, as part of their effort to develop a conventional communication system for David to use, the parents were asked to take on the role of computer programmer for the Dynavox and of creator and maintainer of the hundreds of PECS cards. Nearly a year after I joined them at the university's hospital, David continued to undress himself in places and times deemed inappropriate for a child his age, and his family and team of specialists continued to question the reason. One evening on the phone, Robin described the situation this way: "He didn't come with an instruction booklet." Her comment reflected the frustration she and some of the specialists felt as they struggled to understand and control David's actions.

The following scene illustrates some of the issues David's family had with implementing and coordinating the specialists' recommendations. I was sitting at the kitchen table with Robin while she sorted through a shoe-sized box of hundreds of computer-generated images that previously had been printed, pasted on individual cards, and then laminated with thin, clear plastic film. "We had therapy this morning and we're going to do a picture schedule at home now,"[5] she said with a sigh. "You can never seem to find them [the small strips used for backing or the correct picture] when you need them. . . . We'll need to make at least three of them; one for upstairs, one for in here and one for downstairs." Again, with a sigh, "We're going to have to have a picture schedule because we're going camping this weekend." The family had recently purchased a used camper so they could "do something as a family." Here Robin implied she sought normalcy, to do something normal as a family. The two bulletin boards mounted on the kitchen wall that they used for some picture communication with David were "not very portable, you know." Besides, David often peeled off the Velcro backing and chewed it.

There was a knock on the screen door. "Come in, Sandy. Hi, Sandy," Robin said without stopping her project. Robin introduced us. Sandy and I exchanged greetings while she sat down in the chair beside Robin and set a large three-ring binder on the table that was filled with paperwork Sandy was expected to complete during each visit. Sandy worked for a national service organization as both a respite care provider for David's parents and as David's community support trainer. "We had therapy today," Robin began, telling Sandy about the picture schedule, how cumbersome it was "if you have too many pictures," and how difficult it was to anticipate what pictures one might need for spon-

---

[5] Picture schedules in this case refer to three or four same-sized pictures that are assembled in sequence, to match corresponding activities. The pictures are backed with Velcro and attached to a stiff rectangular piece of paper, like a bookmark, for ease of changing and reuse. For example, Robin might put a picture of a person eating first, followed by a picture of the computer, and then a picture of the toilet. Although David's family sometimes used photographs and black-line computer-generated pictures to tell David who was coming, tell him where they were going, or offer him two pictures from which he could choose a preference, they had previously not used picture schedules at home. School staff, however, regularly used a picture schedule.

taneous communication. Then Robin reported on David's eating and his other activities of the previous night and earlier that morning. "We're using bran for regularity. Yeah, the doctor thought his behavior was based in constipation."

Within a few minutes of my arrival, I had entered into a conversation involving many references to doctors and therapists and specialized language that added to the feeling of separation and stigma. It became clear by Robin's somewhat monotonic speech and the routine nature of their conversation that Robin was well versed in providing people with such reports. Previously, when I had asked Robin about how she felt upon learning of David's diagnosis, she said, "I'm tired of answering that question." Her body language, tone of voice, and the content of what she said confirmed that she was tired— tired perhaps not just physically (she said David had not slept much the previous night) but emotionally from her constant struggle for normalcy in a world of special services that entered her home and dictated much of how their daily home life was supposed to be lived.

As I mentioned earlier, David's relationships with the social and clinical staff were often unequal and unstable, but occasionally people managed to develop shared understanding with him. The social service workers who spent time with David in his home and neighborhood seemed to best illustrate the situation. Sandy was the fifth in a line of social service workers who passed through David's home in less than a few months' time, each one "leaving for different personal reasons," according to Robin. She added, "We walk on eggshells," suggesting that the inconsistency with workers was cause for concern. Their instability also contributed to limiting the opportunities for developing meaningful relationships.

In addition to Sandy, a recent high school graduate named Jenny had worked with David for over a year, but that ended in the fall when she entered a 4-year college where she planned to study special education. Jenny, a friendly young woman, first met David while volunteering in his classroom as part of her high school service program. "My mom told me Robin was looking for someone to do him," she explained. Her comment reflected a discourse where people like David were objects to be *done*, rather than children to be played with. Despite of her language describing her job as it related to David, Jenny also talked about him in ways that suggested she saw him as communicative and intelligent.

One summer day, Jenny sat with me at the kitchen table while David played and occasionally sang along with a computer game. David had chosen one from a collection of educational and instructional software that included Picture It,[6] "Arthur's Birthday" by Marc Brown, and Millie and Bailey Preschool. Jenny described how she and David communicated. "I'm sure Robin has told you that they've got pictures they use," she said. "He uses those so he can choose where to go. We try to use those; sometimes it works

---

[6] Picture It is a computer software program published by the Slater software company. It provides pictures and voice output that students can use to write sentences or stories. It includes options to offer students with a preset vocabulary the chance to select some key words.

and sometimes it doesn't." She explained how they were "working on using sign language some." She continued,

> I think if you're around someone so long, like his little gestures, or like his actions describe what he wants to do or how he feels that day. . . . He has different noises between mad and excited.. . . He pretty much tells, [using] gestures, or goes where he wants to go. . . . If he wants to play on the computer, he'll go over there or if he wants a glass of water, he'll take your hand to get him a glass of water. He understands a lot more than you think. If you just talk to him, if you ask him if he wants to go to the library, he'll shake his head.

Jenny's comments illustrate the subtle nature of communication with David, which she said became easier to understand over time. Her remarks showed features of local understanding, where David's intelligence was recognized, particularly when she said that "He understands a lot more than you think," something she believed becomes evident "if you just talk to him" and if you pay attention to his particular gestures.

Although I did not see them use sign language or the Dynavox during this or subsequent visits, and only rarely did I see Jenny use picture cards to ask David a question, Jenny consistently talked directly to David and he seemed to get his basic needs met while they were together. She referred to him as "Buddy" and she tussled his hair on occasion. She said "Thank you" to David when he let her wipe some pizza sauce from his cheek, when he let her take control of the computer, or when she rubbed his leg to calm him or to rub in lotion. While with Jenny, David often hummed, something she called one of his "content noises." Sandy also constructed shared meaning with David, and in a relatively short period of time, she and David seemed to develop a positive reciprocal relationship that I describe in greater detail later in the chapter.

The only other incident where a clinician seemed to recognize David's intelligence was when his SLP in Hutton talked to me in the waiting room about David. While she discussed the Dynavox with Robin and me, she spoke in hushed tones. "He's listening," she said when she noticed David had looked up from the book he brought with him. Despite believing David was able to understand their discussion about him, the SLP still chose to exclude him from overhearing it

In sum, the social and clinical service system often meant that David was escorted throughout his home and community environments. Much of his time outside of school was spent in therapies or traveling to or from them. The staff and specialists completed large amounts of paperwork documenting David's behaviors. The patterns of interaction between these adults and David were organized in such a way that put the workers in charge of what David was doing, where he was going, and with whom. Also, some of their discourse, particularly when they were out in the community with other worker–client pairs, indicated an uneven power relationship. Jenny's comment about "doin'

David" reflected this reduced status for David. There was an inconsistent use of symbolic communication systems, and combined with David's subtle nature of communication, generative and meaningful interactions appeared limited. Hence, David's social contexts were dominated by people paid to work with him whose jobs included changing David's actions and way of being in the world. Most of these contexts were exclusive (i.e., typically developing children and adults did not go there).

## DAVID AND SCHOOLING: "HE'S PRETTY MUCH IN HIS OWN WORLD."

After summer ended, Robin told me, "He is so happy to be back at school. You should see him . . . jogging down the hall in a body sock." David had been back in school for only a few weeks when I first observed him there. During that visit, the most intriguing interaction occurred during music class, one of the few times when David was integrated with typically developing children. The music teacher was playing songs on a CD and having students pick partners with whom they were to dance. David was not picked as a dance partner for a few rounds, until a small girl, whose top of her head did not even come up to David's shoulder, approached him. Before she had a chance to speak, an associate[7] named Terry asked her, "Do you want to pick David?" "Yeah," the girl answered softly, and the three of them joined the other children in the front of the room, where they stood in two lines with partners facing each other. Terry alternated between modeling for David and physically guiding his movements by standing behind him and holding his hands. When she let go, David stepped across the invisible line and stood immediately beside the girl. She looked up at him for a moment and then resumed the dance, without any apparent concern about his transgression. Then Terry redirected David back to his side, back across the invisible line. Later, David danced alongside the other children when they were allowed to more freely move around the room without any adults directing them.

This vignette captured the struggle David experienced with trying to develop positive relationships within the school context. The music teacher addressed the associate Terry, not David, and Terry seemed to act as a sort of gatekeeper who maintained social borders between David and his classmates by her words and actions. When the little girl approached David, she may have asked him directly to dance if Terry had not anticipated her request. Also, when David crossed the space between the two lines and stood beside the girl, the girl did not seem bothered at all, but Terry redirected him back beside herself. The scene thus represented what continually seemed to be the case for David in school: He was segregated by adult-created social (and sometimes physical) borders, but he and some other children seemed to question and contest those borders.

---

[7] Some of the participants used the word "paraprofessional" to describe teacher assistants whereas others used the word "associate" to mean the same thing. I use them interchangeably.

David's school was situated on the edge of a small town about fifteen miles from his home. Past the lumber yard, the town's waste treatment plant, and a mobile home park stood the small red brick school. It served 4- to 8-year-old children from the surrounding rural community and children up to 12 years old through what Robin called "their severe-profound" special education program. Robin explained that David had been included during his early school years, and she blamed herself for not being able to advocate for more inclusion in recent years. "If you look closely, you will see a correlation between when I returned to work and David's inclusion," meaning that David was more included in school when she had the time to advocate on his behalf.

Roosevelt Elementary was an open school in the sense that there were few walls separating classrooms, with the exception of the special education and specialist (music, art, and physical education) classrooms. "You are always welcome," the principal said after introducing himself. Despite it being an "open school," I found David behind the closed door to one of the special education classrooms. David's special education teacher, Mrs. Sanlon, explained that they kept the door closed because "David has run out of the room this semester." She complained, "I am claustrophobic and I hate keeping my door closed." Mrs. Sanlon was a veteran special education teacher with more than two decades of experience. At the time I visited, she was responsible for six or seven children with significant disabilities. A few of the children used wheelchairs and augmentative and alternative communication (AAC) devices. One boy's feeding tube came out while I was there, and no one was sure how to put it back. "You've gotta have a sense of humor," Mrs. Sanlon told me in the middle of the increasing sense of chaos when an associate tried to find the school nurse and Mrs. Sanlon called the boy's mother to come and help.

Mrs. Sanlon casually introduced me to the three female associates who moved about the room or worked one on one with a child at the rectangular table, making notations on clipboards. Sitting at her desk, typing on the computer, Mrs. Sanlon said to me, "He's taking a break right now. You might get to see something 'cause she [meaning the petite blonde girl beside David] might try to take his toy away." Mrs. Sanlon and I met at the university hospital in the summer, and since then we had conversed briefly via e-mail to set up my visit, so she knew I was interested in David's communication and relationships. She had written, "Communication is an issue. So far this year he has independently asked for food with his Dynavox at snack. Frankly, interaction with others is limited."

David sat with his legs curled up under his bottom. He was barefooted and wearing his plain brown short-sleeved t-shirt and boxer shorts patterned with snowmen. He leaned over the carpet and examined a Disney toy made of a main piece about four inches long with a picture of Belle and the Beast from the movie *Beauty and the Beast*. Several separate small block pieces featuring different character pictures were attached to the main piece by string or thin, flexible wires. He seemed to have taken the toy from among a number of toys in the large, green plastic storage bin situated on the carpet just in front of him. On the opposite side of the bin, a small dark-haired boy wearing leg braces played with another toy. The girl Mrs. Sanlon referred to lay on the floor playing with a plastic school bus. She wore leg braces and the way her back curved backward, I thought she might have cerebral palsy. I asked Mrs. Sanlon whether I could approach David. She responded, "He won't recognize you. He doesn't even seem to recognize his own mom sometimes." Her voice was loud and firm, and it exuded a confidence and authority similar to the way she carried herself about the room.

I approached David. Squatting beside him, I said softly, "Hi, David. I'm Janet. Remember me from your house?" He looked up at me and smiled. When I commented on his toy and touched the picture pieces of Belle in *Beauty and the Beast*, he immediately began to make loud sounds "Ei, Aye," rock back and forth, and shake his hands. David had arranged the pieces, and I realized my touching them troubled him. "I do not want to bother you," I said as I pulled my hand back. "I just want to let you know I am here." I moved back to the large table with the clipboards and sat in a chair. I do not know for certain whether David recognized me, and for a few minutes I did not see much social interaction or communication between David and the other children or adults. But it seemed that several of the children had communication difficulties, and when they did make attempts, sometimes they were discouraged or redirected for being off task. Most of the communication was among the adults, and when they talked to David, it was mostly directive or corrective.

According to David's Individualized Education Program (IEP), 93% of his time was spent in this special education classroom where "Students with similar needs are clustered." Here, Mrs. Sanlon used a combination of specialized educational methods and programs. She primarily used the TEACCH program with David.[8] "Work, play, work, play" was how Mrs. Sanlon described the rhythm of David's school day. For a while, David had been joining a few children in an adjacent special education classroom where they used a literacy program called MEville to WEville,[9] but Robin was told, "David was

---

[8] The Treatment and Education of Autistic and Related Communication Handicapped Children (TEACCH) program is located in the Department of Psychiatry at the University of North Carolina's School of Medicine at Chapel Hill, with several units in other locations. According to their Web site (http://www.teacch.com/), the approach was developed by E. Schopler in the early 1970s to provide "diagnosis and treatment" of autism. "The major priorities," according to the Web site, "include centering on the individual, understanding autism, adopting appropriate adaptations, and a broadly-based intervention strategy building on existing skills and interests." The program is criticized by some people for its misrepresentation as a teaching program rather than as "the behavioral management system" some argue it is and for "its potential use as a tool to restrict and possibly eliminate mainstreaming" (see http://autism-pdd.net/teacch.html).

[9] MEville to WEville is a literacy and communication curriculum published by AbleNet and designed by Karen Erickson, a professor in the Department of Allied Health Sciences at the University of North Carolina. She is also the director of the Center for Literacy and Disability Studies. The program is designed to teach students with significant disabilities about themselves and their relationships to others while also teaching them language, reading, and writing. For further information about the program's effectiveness, see "Toward Positive Literacy Outcomes for Students with Significant Developmental Disabilities," by Erickson et al., available at http://www.atia.org/atob/ATOBWeb/ATOBV2N1/Documents/EricksonATOBV2N1.pdf.

too fast for the others in the group." Again, this suggested another border, even within the special education program.

During my school visits, David followed a short, narrow picture schedule taped to the back of a metal file cabinet beside his wood-topped metal desk. The pictures used with the schedule were black-line drawings with single words describing the drawings generated from the Boardmaker computer program. The pictures that were not being used on the schedule were kept on top of the file cabinet, out of David's reach. The pictures I saw paper-clipped to the schedule strip were for toilet, computer, independent work, and one with David's name. "It works well," Mrs. Sanlon told me. David's desk faced a wall. His name was written on a piece of paper and taped to the top of the chair seat. So although efforts were made using symbol systems to communicate with David, they were extremely limited in content and not generative or readily available to him. Also, the environment and structure of activity seemed to restrict David's opportunities for interesting activities or meaningful communication.

For independent work, David might be given a cardboard box of colored Popsicle sticks or a collection of different sized or shaped objects to sort. Work alone with Mrs. Sanlon was brief (5–10 minutes), and it involved using sign language along with an interactive reading program on the computer or playing a picture-and-sight word-matching game. In these activities, David showed he could read. According to Mrs. Sanlon, "He reads about fifty words." Robin once described a reading assignment Mrs. Sanlon designed where she coded words by using cursive on the back of picture cards but David had quickly cracked the code making it difficult for Robin to complete the homework assignment as Mrs. Sanlon had intended. I did not see how his cursive reading skill was used. During "play" time, David and his classmates were offered the box of toys. On special occasions, the children watched a movie. David might also be offered the chance to get into the body sock, especially if he was jumpy and the adults thought it might help to calm him down. He was allowed to hop or roll around the classroom in the sock. During one of my visits, Mrs. Sanlon told him to do his independent work at his seat while in the sock.

Sometimes David joined one of the associates to run an errand during "play time" or after he had completed his "work." This allowed David some freedom from the routine, and he appeared to enjoy it. I observed the associate Beth ask David whether he wanted to go with her to get a soda in the lounge to bring back for one of the other students. She told David he could take the classroom therapeutic dog along. "He really likes her [the dog]," Beth said. "If you give him the handle, he really likes holding it." During a fire drill, David was calm, according to Beth, because he could walk alongside the dog. David smiled as he walked the dog in the hall and out to the playground for recess, where the dog was clipped to the fence, in view of David. Apparently, the dog barked if David left the play area. Incidentally, when David and his special education classmates went out to recess, they left the building via a separate door than other children. Beth seemed to offer

David one of the few opportunities for interesting, unstructured movement about the school, and she was sensitive to his need for the comfort the dog seemed to afford him.

"He is integrated in 2nd-grade music and PE," Robin wrote to me, "then he has lunch beside the 2nd graders." The 45-minute class periods when David was among children without disabilities, he was accompanied by any one of three associates. In physical education (PE), David towered over the other children as they stood along the wall before being put into groups for a relay race; David was called last to join a group. When I walked across the lunchroom-turned-gymnasium to introduce myself to the PE teacher and briefly explain my project, he responded "Good luck with that" in a cynical tone. His comment seemed to imply that David had no communication or positive relationships. Although this class was considered "integration," I did not see many opportunities for David to interact with his classmates in PE or later when he joined the "regular second-grade class" for 15 minutes of story time. During story time, the teacher read a chapter book from Laura Ingalls Wilder and the children gathered around her on the carpeted floor. Here and in PE, David's associate Terry was almost constantly at his side. During the story, David sat on the edge of the group, leaning back against Terry's legs while she sat in a chair telling him to be quiet. When they stood up after the teacher stopped reading, I overheard Terry say to another boy, "Good job." I asked why she thought he did a "good job," and she answered, "Because he sat by David. You know, they're terrified of him."

Terry seemed to think that David could not manage to build positive relationships with peers or perhaps even with adults. She was quick to say, "He's pretty much in his own world." She and others told me he pinched them, and referring to the children, she said, "They can't trust him not to pinch." However, after further questioning, Terry acknowledged that there were two girls in his class the previous year that walked with him and held his hand. "David hates art," Mrs. Sanlon told me. I asked why and after considering the question for a minute, she said, "Maybe because it's a new teacher or because he was sitting in a new chair, or the fact that he was seated alone, away from the other children." These comments from the people with whom David spent much of his time at school offered conflicting interpretations of David's social interactions. Terry implied that David and his peers were uninterested or unable to successfully build positive relationships, whereas Mrs. Sanlon suggested that David was sensitive to being segregated from his classmates and that he might have wished to build relationships with them. At the same time, Mrs. Sanlon noted that David sat "beside" his classmates at lunch and "alone" in art, which again reinforced his separateness rather than integration.

My observations, like the previous description of David's music class illustrated, resonated with Mrs. Sanlon's reflective analysis that David (and I would add that also his peers) sought out social interactions. His occasional acting in parallel to his classmates rather than with them might be more of a result of their physical separation or the influence of some adult attitudes and behaviors rather than circumstances resulting from David's direct interactions with his classmates. Although David and his classmates did not regularly use words or pictures to interact directly, they remained somewhat curious about each other. As I described, David crossed the space between the two lines of children in music to dance beside his partner. The previous year he walked hand in hand with some classmates. He allowed classmates to join him in his body sock and tunnel. Mrs. Sanlon told me that a second grader, seemingly undismayed by learning that David did not talk, asked whether David could use sign language because she knew some signs.

Furthermore, according to David's K–1 teacher, where he was more fully included, he had developed some positive reciprocal relationships. "[David] really liked a little boy named Paul who was very patient with him and [who] would take David's hand when we went on walks." She added, "He also liked Tammy and she would come into our room and read a book." Both David's teacher and his mother agreed that he had a positive relationship with the associate during those early years; the teacher wrote, "David really really connected with [her]."

Music class seemed to offer David the greatest opportunity for social interaction in school; it was a less structured environment, where interaction was encouraged, and sometimes spontaneous, less conventional movements were not viewed as deviant. Although they were limited, David's positive interactions with his classmates and with some of the adults suggested something other than someone "in his own world." Perhaps the happiness David's mother sensed upon his return to school in the fall was happiness borne out of the social interactions beyond his family and his own hope for renewed opportunities for social and intellectual growth. He and his classmates and to some extent a few adults in his school seemed to question, if not challenge, the social borders that controlled and dominated David's experiences in this context.

## DAVID'S HOME LIFE: "DAVID HAS OPENED UP DIFFERENT DOORS FOR US."

In contrast to school, David was frequently part of the flow of social interactions in his home. He seemed to move freely around the house and yard, occasionally entering into brief exchanges with others. He played with his siblings and parents. He also seemed to carefully watch them and others who came into the home. As the opening scene to this chapter showed, he is viewed by his family as a valued member. As a family, they typically ate together at the kitchen table and attended Sunday services at their church. During the summer and holiday vacations, they traveled to visit extended relatives or regional places of interest. Upon entering the wider community, however, David, and by extension his family, met varying degrees of acceptance, about which David's parents seemed particularly sensitive. In a sense, they became entangled in the social restrictions some of the wider community set on David.

At home, David sometimes played computer games or puzzles with his siblings. They rode bikes and took hikes together. "He's playing more with his brother and sister,"

Jenny, the respite care provider, reported. "With Anastasia," Robin explained, "She's affectionate. She wants to hug him. She wants to kiss him. She wants love or a bond with him. [Bobby] is like any 7-year-old boy; he wants his brother to play with him." Like his brother and sister, sometimes David was left alone to read books or play with his cards, toys, or the computer. At these times, his family members addressed him in passing. His parents also greeted him upon first seeing him after school with a hug and "Hi, David." They sometimes asked the other children directly how school was and then looked through David's backpack for clues as to how his school day was. They also asked Sandy, who met the school van each afternoon at the local elementary school to take David home, about his day and to report on what she learned from the van driver.

Robin and Dan both spoke fondly about David's early years. They joined their children in laughter when they shared the family photo album. Dan reminisced, "When David was about 1½ years old, he would line up Barbie doll shoes. [It] is a common theme. I remember early on he'd turn on the water," and the teachers wanted him to stop, "so he'd have to ask first. He overgeneralized. [Now] he'll just stand there or he'll lead you [to the faucet or the TV]." Dan appeared mixed in his interpretations of David's role within the family. On one occasion, when they had several female visitors over, Dan included David along with Bobby as "one of the boys" who might need to escape all the women by going outside. He regularly cuddled and affectionately wrestled with David. At the same time, Dan referred to his son's diagnosis as a neurological disorder and discussed autism in terms of something that needed a cure.

When David was an infant, Robin became part of a long-term study about mother–child relationships; this was before David was given a diagnosis. The study involved periodic videotaping sessions, and during one of my visits to their home, I joined the family in viewing the tape. In one video clip, an 18-month-old David sat in his mom's lap while she read one of Eric Carle's board books to him. "He loves books," Bobby interrupted. I had heard this before from several different people: David's K–1 teacher, the respite care providers who took him to the library, and from his mother. I noticed David reading[10] a book by the large glass doors one morning, and Robin told me that was what he usually did on weekends. I watched David sort through stacks of books on the upstairs landing, where he identified books of particular series and put them together. David often brought books with him in the bathroom while using the toilet, on car rides, and to therapy. Thus, Bobby's comment and the video showed that David's interest in books had developed early in his life.

For about 5 minutes during the video viewing, I drew the 10-year-old David's movements. He was constantly moving but keeping his eye mostly on the TV. He walked up to the TV, then back behind my chair, then to the glass doors, then back behind me, over

---

[10] I do not know if David was reading in the conventional sense, but his IEP states, "David currently receptively reads 73 words."

near his brother, back to the TV, behind me again, to the doors, and back behind me again, where he paused for a while. He looked at the tape and then to his mom, who sat in the chair beside me. "He sees me," she said aloud, before turning her gaze back to the TV. David smiled when his mother spoke about him, and his calmed body seemed to indicate a sense of contentment. A few minutes later, after eating cut up pieces of toast for a snack upstairs in the kitchen, I noticed David looking again at the TV through the staircase banisters and humming; he appeared to be content in this context.

Despite identifying her family as "transplants," Robin told me she felt they were "accepted" by their congregation and some people in the community. In reference to David's unconventional communication and behavior, Robin said, "I guess with some of them [at church] you feel a connection just because I think they truly understand or are aware of the idiosyncrasies of it." She went on to describe why she felt comfortable within the church community and how her family benefited from David's membership:

> You don't have to hide how things really are or put on a fake . . . [pause] minimize things, hide things. Like the disrobing, or you know, I have scars on my arm because he has scratched me, not to hide that. . . . I think you get your ties through your kids, and David has opened up different doors for us.

In addition to members of their church, Robin offered the school bus driver and the librarian as examples of people in the community with whom they had developed positive relationships through initial contact with David. She said she had met other children in the community through David as well. "Even when we were trick or treating, kids said hi to David. I'm used to them saying hello to Bobby, but some [children she did not know] said hello to David." Robin added that she and "Dan are probably better teachers because of David. We have more understanding for families with a kid that comes in who is struggling." Although both Robin and Dan openly discussed their frustrations with how David's behavior seemed to restrict their own social experiences in the wider community, Robin's comments show how she viewed her son as a contributing member to their family.

David and his family usually spent holidays at church functions and with extended family. Robin said they saw her side of the family only "maybe three times a year," but more frequently they visited Dan's relatives, who seemed to be more comfortable with David. "[He] communicates with Dan's mom and lets her know if he needs something. And he responds to her." By comparison, Robin told me in an irritated tone, her own parents usually did not address David directly, and they told her more than once that she should "send him away." Thus, David's interactions with extended family varied considerably, and the idea that family might not accept David clearly upset his parents.

Although Robin and Dan seemed to resent the negative responses from some of the extended family, they also appeared to understand why some people had these reactions. They frequently struggled with trying to get David dressed. They both told me about the difficulty David sometimes had sleeping, how he woke up and turned on the bathroom water, how he had broken things like the toilet paper roll, and how his sometimes unusual behaviors led to self-imposed restrictions regarding their entire family's social plans. One evening when I phoned, I found David's father cleaning up one of David's messes. First he blamed himself: "I must've left him too long [on the computer]. I should've picked up clues." Then he suggested the reason David urinated on himself might have been because "He had gotten locked up," meaning David was so focused on the computer he had not noticed he needed to relieve himself. Finally, after changing the topic briefly to his other son, Bobby, and saying he was "above average," Dan sighed and said, "It's an imperfect world."

David's parents purposefully did not plan vacations that included places or activities they thought would upset David, but sometimes they were not able to accurately anticipate other people's reactions to him. For instance, on more than one occasion, they had been asked to leave different museums. According to Robin, sometimes they were told to leave for "making too much noise" or "when David is excited and he starts doing, you know, his little skip." In some cases, they felt the need to apologize to strangers who they thought might misinterpret David's behavior. They seemed to feel it was not always worth the social embarrassment to even try to go out into the community, thus self-restricting their activities. Robin said that when people stared, "I think they thought he shouldn't have been in there. I was tired of explaining." Also, they expressed concern that David's needs and behaviors sometimes restricted his siblings' social experiences. In an effort to address this concern, for the first time in their lives, David's family had left him with a respite care provider overnight while they went to a water park. Afterward, Robin felt guilty about it.

The summer following the beginning of my study, Robin informed me that "in order to keep David safe," they had decided to place him in a supervised group home. He had left the house in the night, and they thought they had lost him. "It is a horrible decision for us," Robin wrote me, "but for David's safety, we need help." She explained that two more support staff had quit. "We just can't take the risk that Anastasia or Bobby would forget to lock the door, David would get out and lost, and they would blame themselves for the rest of their lives." It seemed that the combination of insufficient supports and concerns about risking the other children's guilt was more than David's parents could take on; the social stigmatization of David in the wider community, it could be argued, also contributed to their decision.

Overall, David's home life included affection and membership but not without tension that emerged from engaging in the wider social community. His family addressed him directly and respectfully. His siblings played with him, and his younger brother enjoyed sharing a bedroom with him. When David was given alone time, he chose to go on the computer, play cards or put together puzzles, or read books. David joined his family on many excursions, including church, camping, and museums, where they were met with mixed responses of acceptance and rejection. Thus, although David's family viewed him as a contributing member, they also increasingly questioned their capabilities for handling the level of risk involved with keeping him at home. As part of the next section shows, David developed positive reciprocal relationships with his family, but these seemed somewhat tenuous when taken into consideration with how David was soon moved out of his home.

## WAYS OF KNOWING DAVID

*FIGURE 3. Anastasia's drawing—"David and I hugging."*

*FIGURE 4. Bobby's drawing—"We're playing in his [blue] body sock."*

David developed some positive reciprocal relationships even though he had not yet developed a complex conventional form of communication. In this section, I focus on David's relationships with the special education teacher Mrs. Sanlon, Sandy the social service worker, and his mother and siblings. His relationship with Mrs. Sanlon seemed to provide some insight into a way of knowing David that included some, but certainly not all, features of local understanding and positive interactions. She appeared to have difficulty challenging the social borders that her position had in a way created. By contrast, the social service worker Sandy, who—like the teacher, held a position of authority and worked within a system that oftentimes emphasized David's differences—interacted with and talked about David in more respectful and humanizing ways. Sandy empathized with David in much the same way as David's mother, Robin, did; they both imagined life from his perspective. Along with their mother, David's siblings hugged and played with him (see Figures 3 and 4). All of these relationships reinforced David as an intelligent and sensitive human being.

## MRS. SANLON: "HE'S GONE AND MADE A LIAR OUT OF ME."

Although it was within a specialized educational system where difference meant deviance, Mrs. Sanlon's relationship with David exhibited some feature of local understanding. She seemed to recognize David as an intelligent human being when she said, "He's got more on his mind than we can ever know" and "He's not functioning up to the level of his mind." She indicated her interest in seeking ways of successfully communicating with David by investing her own time outside of the regular work schedule to consult so-called experts in the field of autism. On the day when Mrs. Sanlon informed me that David would not recognize me because he often did not even recognize his own mother, she later recanted. I sat with David and Mrs. Sanlon at the lunch table when David's mother appeared. David looked up from his food and reached his hand out to his mom as she joined us. Mrs. Sanlon then openly admitted her previously articulated low expectations: "He's gone and made a liar out of me." Such an admission illustrates how, to a certain, extent she recognized David's ability to dispel negative stereotypes.

Additionally, Mrs. Sanlon appeared to recognize David as a person with needs similar to herself and others. One day she offered three reasons why David might scratch: "One, he's frustrated, trying to tell us something, but just doesn't have the words. Two, he just doesn't want to do it, the work or whatever it is. Or three, he wants something and he just doesn't have the words to tell us what it is." These reasons bear a remarkable resemblance to the reasons any of us have for acting out frustrations in ways that others, even those most close to us, might not immediately understand or find reasonable.

Like Robin, Mrs. Sanlon expressed hope that David would someday develop conventional communication, preferably speech, but other forms of more reliable and conventional communication seemed an acceptable alternative. "I want him to be able to tell me [his thoughts]," she said. She described his use of sign language as idiosyncratic, "So it's almost useless for social interaction." She argued, "If you need an interpreter or you can't generalize your signs . . . you can't be understood." She sounded more hopeful that David would become proficient with the Dynavox. "He's using it more. He requests food a lot better than last year," and "[he uses it] to pick playthings." Mrs. Sanlon's efforts to develop a more sophisticated way to communicate with David focused around changing David's behaviors. This perspective of their relationship—that he needed to change rather than she—might suggest something other than a positive reciprocal relationship.

Despite the often tough, impersonal, and occasional outright negative attitudes of some adults responsible for David's education, there were also times when some of these same people talked and acted in ways that might be considered more respectful. Robin expressed the belief that Mrs. Sanlon and the associate Beth were the people at school who best understood David. Robin thought that Mrs. Sanlon "knows her stuff," and so Robin placed her trust in Mrs. Sanlon's expertise. Regarding Beth, Robin wondered aloud, "I'm not sure [why she understands David]. She just knows." I observed Beth share some of her own lunch with David and offer to take David out on an errand. Her tone of voice was always calm, not authoritative or patronizing, when she talked to David. "He can tell you what he likes," Beth told me. "Books, movies." Mrs. Sanlon interjected, "He wants them all." The manner in which these two women talked about and interacted with David suggested a mixture of respect for him as a fellow human being with interests and preferences, as well as someone who they thought just did not fit in the regular social context of school.

Mrs. Sanlon suspected David was far more capable than what she thought he showed openly, but like her approach to his communication, she thought David was responsible for this apparent lack of performance. She expressed her opinion that he did not try hard enough to live up to her expectations, which seemed to cause her a good deal of frustration. She did not offer a preferred or alternative program to that in which she worked (discreet trial format and applied behavioral analysis), nor did she bring up ideas about how to include David more or how she might do things differently in an effort to help bring his talents to the surface.

The IEP Mrs. Sanlon wrote only briefly referenced what might be considered one of David's strengths: "[He] has gained some independence." The few of David's preferences that were included were described as useful "motivators" for teachers to "use" with David: "Candy, salty foods, computer time, Disney books/movies/audiotapes, and musical toys continue to be good *motivators* to use with David" (italics added). The dominant focus of the IEP was on David's behavioral conformity. The functional behavioral assessment (FBA) included in the IEP suggested the reason for David's pinching was to "escape work, waiting, [and] tasks he doesn't desire." "When demands are put upon David to do a task or to wait for a task to start," the FBA stated, he pinched himself or other people. He might also pinch, it noted, "in situations that are out of the routine." The FBA described the reason for David's pinching as a need to "escape," but the school staff did not "allow" him to escape. Instead they were expected to find ways to get David back to the task at hand. The plan to reduce David's pinching listed the following:

"timer—tangibles, help card, training in help on the Dynavox, continue to reinforce the use of help sign. David's behaviors were tabulated and displayed in various graph forms. In this way, Mrs. Sanlon's understanding of David and the possibility of developing local understanding seemed to be limited.

One situation I observed and found interesting was where Mrs. Sanlon interpreted David's nonverbal communication and then gave it a voice. David sat cross-legged on his chair one day at school with his fingers in his ears, Mrs. Sanlon said to him, "You're mad. What's ya mad about? You want me to go?" Although she did not use first-person (like Robin and Sandy did) to give David a voice, she was voicing her interpretations of David's behavior in a way I think begins to show features of local understanding in communication with David where his actions were viewed as meaningful. Similarly, Terry the associate said to a passing adult, "He's angry," when David squealed "Ee aa ooa," in the hallway. Here, she acted like a language interpreter for the other adult who she seemed to think needed to understand that David's vocalizations were indeed communication.

Although Mrs. Sanlon valued David's intelligence, she seemed to reflect a school culture where David was viewed as someone in control of himself who needed to change his behaviors (keep his clothes on, not scratch, and use the Dynavox or other AAC) before he would be allowed further access to general education environments and the people who reside there. Furthermore, it was unclear how David's intelligence and interests would be used to develop his communication and literacy skills. David's reading goal was to increase his reading vocabulary from the baseline of 70 words to 100 words. In sum, David's relationship with his special education teacher illustrated a few features of local understanding (e.g., seeing intelligence), but she did not presume his right to membership among his typically developing peers.

## DAVID AND SANDY: SEEKING MEMBERSHIP

It was interesting to observe Sandy and David negotiate meaning and develop a relationship at the same time I was coming to know him. Regardless of cautious tales she may have heard from previous support service workers and her own experience with David disrobing and running away from her in town, as Robin said with relief, "Sandy didn't give up." Sandy said she was "bound and determined" to come to understand David. After having worked with David for about 4 months, she described the importance of mutual trust and acceptance in their relationship:

> I would say like the last two weeks I think there's finally a really . . . [she paused]. I
> see a decent connection between David and I. I mean, you know, there always was
> somewhat, but he's like more trusting and sort of like I'm fitting in as one of the
> members of his family. I mean, not of course quite as close. I mean, I can see with
> them, you know, he just . . . [Her voice faded while she thought for a minute]. Like

with Robin, where he'll run right over . . . if I ask him if I can have a hug, he will come back up to me and do that now.

Indeed, before she left that day, Sandy and David exchanged hugs. Sandy said that both of them were "more comfortable" with each other, after spending time together. More important, however, Sandy raised the point here that David's acceptance of her was crucial to their relationship, thus addressing the aspect of its reciprocity. Like me, she saw ways in which David was an accepted member of his family, and she sought David's acceptance as crucial to her own acceptance as a sort of family member.

When I pointed to Sandy's photograph from among several on the kitchen table, David looked up at Sandy who was then talking on the phone, indicating recognition. One time, according to Robin, she showed David Sandy's picture to assure him Sandy was coming, and "he smiled and jumped." Sandy always talked gently and directly to David. Like Jenny, the high school respite worker, Sally rubbed his legs to calm him and she began advocating for him. As an advocate, she asked the other children to quiet down when David squealed loudly and put his fingers in his ears, indicating his frustration. She also cautioned Anastasia against offering him soda or letting him near the candles.

Sandy seemed to view David as intelligent. She whispered when she talked to me about him and thought he might have been in hearing range. "He understands every-thing," she whispered, then added, almost as an afterthought, "*I* believe. But it's hard for him verbally." By qualifying her assertion that David understood everything when she added "*I* believe," Sandy might have been deferring to the specialists' view, showing some reticence from affirming what she thought was a shared understanding with David. Yet time and again I saw her talk to him, and he acknowledged her verbalization with a nod, a vocalization, or a more conventional form of nonverbal communication, like pointing. "He knows what you're saying," she said again. "I just sorta know his ways." She also indicated that sometimes David's intentions were obvious, such as the time she took out the Dynavox and asked him what he wanted; he pressed the "shut down" button and shoved it away. "When he put it away, Janet, it's a pretty good indication, I mean, I'm just assuming that it's a 'No.'"

Sandy also came to know David's food preferences and interests. "He loves to take everything apart. . . . You know, I been around him long enough to pick up what his likes and dislikes are. Not everything though, but most of the time. You know, sorta sense it." Her comments reflect a thoughtful and perceptive interpretation of David as an intel-ligent and sensitive person, and she talked about his differences as "his ways" rather than something that needed changing or that meant such deviance as to define him.

When Sandy talked to me about David, she showed empathy. She described what she said was one of the rare times when "He's really stressing," when he may be crying and pacing "really hard." She said it might be like a "bad headache, or you know, something's hurting on him." She always interpreted his behavior as meaningful. At times, David crawled under the desk in the kitchen. "It's for security. It's his own little spot," she explained. Earlier she had told me, "Sometimes he just likes his own space." While sitting on the floor outside the upstairs bathroom waiting for David to finish reading his book while on the toilet, Sandy suggested to me that maybe he liked her because she "just kind of let him do his own thing." She made it clear she did not mean she let him do anything he wanted. Instead, she indicated that she let him know she accepted him for who he was.

## ROBIN: "CAN YOU IMAGINE WHAT IT WOULD BE LIKE?"

My observations of David with his family at home, where he moved about with confidence and joy, suggested he was well cared for and loved. He regularly sought out (and was given) physical comfort from his parents and siblings. David climbed into his mother's lap as she sat on the floor where they cuddled and tumbled around, both laughing. Upon coming home from work, David's father took off his coat and immediately climbed the stairs, where he took David into his arms. They sat on a chair in the hallway, David twisting and turning upside down, his head touching the floor and facing out, his legs wrapped around his father's chest. Or when David was in his body sock, Dan stuck his head inside it as well, joining his son in squeals of laughter, "OO EE AA." Dan popped his head back out and said to me, "He likes it." David's elder sister, Anastasia, said she knew when David's vocalizations meant he wanted a kiss or a hug (see Figure 3). She wrote a caption for her drawing: "David and I hugging. David only hugs me. He hugs me after school." Later she told me, "He loves me." Anastasia told me that when David put his hands over his ears, "He doesn't want to talk." Robin explained that David makes a certain sound sequence when he is referring to Anastasia. Bobby said, "I feel like I know him most in my family." He offered rational reasons for David's unusual behaviors, suggesting that David took his clothes off when he got hot. These interactions and comments were reflective of the positive way of knowing David his family enjoyed.

One of the most powerful examples of how David's family interacted with and interpreted David became evident when I transcribed what David and his family said on the digital voice recorder I gave them to take on one of their camping trips. I would hear a voice, something indistinguishable, presumably from David, followed by Robin saying, "As you heard, David sees a trolley." She narrated a description of the different scenes: "David is sitting and happily clapping and watching a roller coaster." Bobby's then 6-year-old voice announced, "David's happy. We're all having fun . . . . Janet, I wish you could be here because we're having so much fun."

One of the more poignant things Robin described on the recorder was an interaction she had with David at the end of their trip:

> At the end of our hike, he looked at me and he smiled, jumping and clapping. He was just . . . [she paused]. He looks deep in your eyes and he kind of leans forward

like, "Oh, I'm so excited! Look at me!" Oh, actually I got a hug when we were walking
along. He squeezed tight. So, I guess that's his communication.

These voiced interpretations, like when Robin imagines David's voice saying, "Oh, I'm
so excited! Look at me!," recognized David as a legitimate equal partner in specific communicative interactions. They also provided him with an opportunity to become a member of the wider social community.

David's family members regularly adjusted their own behaviors to include David in
their social interactions. Anastasia said that David liked to ride bikes, so she took him
for rides on the back of their tandem. Both she and her mother yielded to David when
he pulled on their shoulders seeking a piggyback ride. When their parents told David's
younger brother, Bobby, that they were planning on moving them into separate bed-
rooms, Bobby refused, saying he wanted David to stay his roommate. Apparently, David's
nighttime antics were not enough of a reason in Bobby's mind to warrant David's removal
from the bedroom. Bobby and David played together with puzzles, on the computer or
in David's body sock (see Figure 4).

In addition to loving David and incorporating him in the family's interactive flow,
Robin articulated a more complex understanding of what it might be like to be her
son. One warm late summer Sunday afternoon, she shared that understanding with me.
Bobby and Anastasia were playing in the neighbor's backyard with the neighbor's daughter. One could easily hear their laughter and the occasional sound of the neighbor's
llamas in the field nearby. Dan was walking the perimeter of their 7-acre plot of land,
checking on the health of the 100 or so tree seedlings he had recently planted. Sitting on
the wooden deck chair while David walked back and forth alongside the railing eyeing
his siblings, Robin imagined life from David's perspective:

> We have noticed that he gets upset if we go where he doesn't expect us to go . . .. If we
> got in the car and we looked like we were going to go to a friend's house, but we didn't,
> boy that made him mad. [She paused.] It would be odd living your life not knowing
> where you were going and when we were going, what we were doing; just following
> along. [Again, she paused.] It would drive me nuts.

It was clear that Robin thoughtfully reflected on David's life experiences. More than a
month later, Robin again put herself in David's position when she asked rhetorically,
"Can you imagine what it would be like if everybody gets in the car, but you have no
idea of where you are going?" By imagining life from David's perspective, Robin openly
expressed his right to an emotional status equal to her own. In other words, she recognized David's right to express frustration with his circumstances, and thus she elevated
his social status to one similar to her own. Her comments then illustrated the nature of
reciprocity in positive relationships of local understanding, where the person without the

demonstrable difference interprets the person with the disability, in this case David, as someone who experiences life much like the rest of us, as human beings.

Repeatedly Robin seemed to call for a reinterpretation of her son from how others viewed him. She especially struggled with stereotypical interpretations of people the larger society considered to be socially deviant. For instance, she described an ongoing frustration she and Dan experienced with their pastor, who they learned was talking and dressing in such a disheveled way as to suggest he was "a retard." When they first complained to him, the pastor said it was an effective way to get kids' attention. When they followed up their complaint with a letter pointing out the hypocrisy of using denigrating stereotypes in an effort to teach children about Christianity, the pastor agreed to stop using the props and characterization. It was ironic that the pastor of the church where Robin said she thought David was accepted was using negative stereotypes to the congregation's youth. On a number of occasions, she referred to some school personnel's attitudes as degrading as well. "You know, he's not garbage," she said in response to such intolerance and lack of understanding.

After reading Kluth's (2003) book about children with autism, titled *You're Going to Love This Kid*, Robin told me, "I feel exactly like her, 'Look at the kid, not at his disability.'" David's relationship with his immediate family seemed complicated by a tension that surfaced when other people did not recognize David's value as an individual human being and as one who warranted membership within various social contexts. Robin's advocacy for David's membership, where she argued for others to "look at the kid," seemed to have developed out of a particularly positive way of knowing David that included a deeper understanding of how David might experience the world.

*A Search for David's Worldview*

My efforts to capture David's worldview proved to be particularly challenging because, in part, we did not have shared histories, nor did we share a system of communication. In fact, the people with whom David seemed to share understanding continued to question their interpretations, frequently answering "I don't know" to my queries about David's meaning. There was a general atmosphere surrounding David's communication that suggested people were always guessing at his meaning. At the same time, people familiar to him often verbalized their interpretations of his intended meaning. When I told people that I intended to informally interview David, they were surprised. Robin said that no one had ever sought David's perspective before.

Although David had some success with using various forms of conventional communication, such as voiced speech, sign language, pointing to pictures and words, and using the Dynavox, these were inconsistently used and not readily available for different reasons. As such, the process of capturing David's perspective was complicated by the difficulty of establishing a shared mode of communication. In an effort to address this issue,

I revisited the words and advice from people who shared similar features of autism and from people who have studied their movement and communication differences (Biklen, 2005; Crossley, 1997; Gillingham & McClennen, 2003; Grandin, 2005; Kluth, 2004; Williams, 1994). Their suggestions included presuming competence (Biklen & Burke, 2006), careful listening (Lovett, 1996), and waiting for the person's attention before speaking (Donnellan, Leary, & Robledo, 2006). Therefore, when interpreting David's actions and words, I assumed that David was a competent person with thoughts and feelings similarly to my own and that I needed to become particularly sensitive to how David communicated those thoughts and feelings.

The following excerpt from my field notes describes a typical summer day for David at home where I began to more clearly see ways in which David communicated with others. The scene shows how David sometimes chose to spend his time when the weather outside was unpleasant. On this day, David had chosen to play with his new cards his siblings had bought for him during their recent camping trip. He might just as likely have chosen to sit with a book and read by the light of the glass door or to play with an interactive educational computer game or his Thomas the Train wooden train set, all activities he has chosen to do during his free time at home.

Bobby was stacking and counting his money from his pink, plastic piggy bank, and Anastasia was creating a tower of rejected videotapes, searching for one she wanted to show me. After helping Bobby and talking with him and his sister for awhile, I stood up and said I was going upstairs to see David. Before I left them, I noticed a 12-inch blue plastic ball with bumps all over it that sat in the corner, and I asked the kids whether they thought David might like to play with it. "Yeah, that's one of his favorites," Bobby replied. So I took the ball upstairs with me, and I bounced it lightly so David could hear me coming before he could see me.

David was sitting with his bare feet curled under his bottom. He wore boxer shorts and a t-shirt. I did not say anything when I approached the top of the stairs. Rather, I sat down in the hall a couple of feet away from David, beside the banisters that overlooked the landing where the other kids were playing. I began rolling the ball into the overflowing bookshelf and letting it roll back to me, waiting to see whether David might engage me. With his back against the wall, David and I faced the same direction. He had a pile of his oval-shaped playing cards, all face down, and one by one he picked them up and set them down in rows of five or six cards in front of himself. He rocked occasionally, then stopped and put a card down beside another one. "Eer . . . eeree," he hummed quietly to himself.

David's bedroom was to his left, and I could see in it. I noticed the new wooden bed frame his parents were given from friends the day before. A homemade quilt stretched out on top of the unmade bed. Above his headboard on the wall next to the light switch were two laminated pictures with the words "light" and "sleep" written on them. Beyond David, between his bed and his brother's junior bunk bed, and in front of the window, was a very large green plastic "therapy" ball.

Before more than a few quiet minutes had passed, before I felt I had any chance to see whether David might become interested in the ball I had, Anastasia appeared in the doorway. She insisted, rather loudly, that we join her in the basement to watch a video.[11] In what seemed to me to be a somewhat rough movement, Anastasia bent down and tried to pick David up. It looked like he resisted, but she was a big, strong girl. I asked her to stop and assured her that David would come on his own if he wanted. She agreed to use the picture I retrieved from the kitchen wallboard showing the TV, but she persisted in holding onto David for a few minutes, until she let go and led me downstairs, allowing David to come on his own terms.

This scene illustrates several features of a typical summer day for David. He was given some time to freely engage in an activity that gave him pleasure. David's humming and absence of obvious tension while playing with the cards his siblings had given him seemed to indicate a sense of contentedness. Books and other symbolic forms of communication (e.g., the word cards on the wall and the images and numerals on the cards) were all part of his daily experience, and they might have served as a more accessible and comfortable conduit for communication for David than did direct conversation if his experience with sensory integration was similar to those to whom I referred above who share the autism label. David's freedom to remain alone or to move about by his own will was sometimes thwarted by others, as in my initial interruption (and that of other therapists, behavioral specialists, or researchers) and Anastasia's subsequent interruption and physical handling. The scene did not, however, illustrate many of David's more obvious communicative efforts, both verbal and nonverbal, to socially connect with others, something that became more evident after reviewing several months of field notes and other document data.

Before I describe David's communication in detail, however, I want to note David's interest in photographs and visual images and how I used this interest to try to learn more about him. Earlier I described how David was drawn to the family photo album. Another time I found him studying family pictures as he pulled stacks of them from shoeboxes, held them in his hand, and then set them out on the floor. So one day I arrived with a felt board and a collection of felt pieces on some of which I had already glued pictures of my own family members. I showed David the felted photos and talked about my family (making it into a story about my husband baking bread, something Robin did regularly) as I placed them on the feltboard. David spent several minutes with me looking at them and moving them on the board. Shortly thereafter I glued photos of David and each of his family members on their own pieces of felt. After I left, David spent several minutes moving his family photos in different sequenced orders. Another time I laid out

---

[11] This was the video I referred to previously, where David and his mother were videotaped as part of a longitudinal study about families of children attending Head Start. Anastasia was equally interested in showing the video to me as well as in seeing herself in it as a toddler.

large pieces of paper on the floor and offered David the opportunity to draw with some markers. He did not join me and his mother until after she began to draw a portrait of David (see Figure 1) and wrote his name underneath. Then, in parallel, David drew a similarly sized shape that looked like a head, and then he added marks that resembled facial features like a nose and mouth (see Figure 2). When David's mother presumed he was drawing her and she began to write her name under it, David immediately jumped up and began hopping, shaking his hands, and making high-pitched sounds. We interpreted this to mean that she was wrong to assume he was drawing her, and when Robin crossed out her own name and wrote David's own name, he calmed down and rejoined us. This seemed a strong indication that David sought recognition for his work and had a sense of personal identity. It also showed how he negotiated meaning with Robin.

Although David typically used few verbal or written words to express himself, he often communicated his interest in and affection toward others nonverbally. Sandy said, "He likes to cuddle," after having known him only for a few weeks. I observed David kiss his mother and his sister. When wading in the lake one summer day, he progressively floated nearer some kids his age who were swimming and playing in the water. At the library when he saw one of his classmates, David went up to her and hugged her. Similarly in school contexts, like in music class or during book sharings, David sought out contact with peers. In one therapy session, after bringing the picture schedule up to his lips, he turned and looked intently at me. He then gently raised his fingers to my lips. Then he did the same thing to the therapist. "Yes," she said to David, acknowledging his communication, "two of us." Over the months I spent with David, it became customary for him to slide his fingers over my open hand as part of our greeting ritual or when I said "good-bye." Once he pulled my hands together to Robin's and Sandy's hands, and then he smiled. I interpreted these exchanges as his acknowledgement of me and assent for our developing relationship.

In addition to lightly touching hands with other people, David gazed into the other person's eyes for exaggerated moments of time. "In April we didn't have that [eye contact]," Robin said, suggesting that David's communication was becoming increasingly complex. "The eye contact really improved since school let out." On several occasions, I observed David and his mother seek each other out and interact in this affectionate, affirming way, gently touching hands and gazing into each other's eyes. He also interacted with me in this way both at home and at school. These nonverbal forms of communication showed David's interest in others in ways similar to but not always consistent with other people labeled with autism. In other words, David's actions communicated some preferences to be with, to touch, and to share eye gazes with other people. In this way, he, like others labeled autistic, seemed to dispel the "myth of the person alone" (Biklen, 2005). Of equal importance is how David's increased eye contact seemed to differ from that of some other people labeled autistic (Donnella, Leary, & Robelo, 2006; Kluth, 2004), suggesting the nature of his individual differences within such a "group."

David regularly vocalized in his efforts to communicate with others, oftentimes making combinations of speech sounds that seemed to repeat themselves. Both Robin and Mrs. Sanlon told me, "We're getting more vocalizations." David's voiced sounds were usually interrupted with pauses, but most of the time, he blended his sounds together. Even after listening to the voice recorder repeatedly, I still could not decipher any familiar words, so I transcribed David's vocalizations phonetically as "EEE" or "EEEiiiooo," using capital letters to indicate an increase in volume. When vocalizing, David tended to begin loudly, especially when he appeared excited or upset. If David was addressed directly, he regularly responded with a vocalization. For example, upon arriving at his house, I would find David and say, "Hi, David," at which point he often said "EEE." Once when Sandy arrived and greeted David, Robin prompted him to respond by saying "Hel-lo" in a sort of stilted way. David did then respond with "Burrr . . . eeee."

In therapy, David appeared to enter into a sort of dialogue whereby his therapist said something to him and he responded using what would be the socially appropriate cadence and inflection. After the therapist said "Thank you" to him, David replied "Eeeya, eeeya." Regarding David's vocalizations, the SLP said it often takes her time and reflection to decipher what she thinks David was intending to say. But she told me that she often determined that he was meaningfully communicating with her. In these ways, when David was recognized verbally, he often responded verbally, just not using conventional or recognizable words.

Occasionally David did voice words that were perceptible and distinguishable to others. His mother and Jenny, the respite care provider, said that David likes to sing and that he knows all the words, like those in the Beatles' song "Yellow Submarine" and many of the Disney songs. When playing with his father one late afternoon, he repeated "Dad, Dad, Dad, Dad." In this case, the word "Dad" seemed to flow from his mouth without much effort. However, at other times, it looked as though producing speech took great effort and concentration on David's part, where he struggled to push the words out. After we witnessed one of these incidences, David's father said in a resigned sort of way, "I don't see the good in forcing a person to talk who doesn't want to." It was unclear whether Dan's comment was an expression of his own frustration with understanding David's inconsistency with producing conventional speech or whether he thought David was not able to use speech and so they should not try to expect him to. Once during Sunday church services, while sitting beside his mother, David suddenly said aloud and with clarity, "I love you, Mom."

Robin explained how for David "The words get stuck [in his throat]." I observed this phenomenon a few times in his home when someone asked David a question. He stopped, turned to face the person who spoke, took a breath, and then slowly and carefully formed his mouth and lips before exhaling and producing sounds. His efforts seemed to exhaust him. Sometimes David moved his mouth, but no sound came out. Jenny said that for David, "It's like, come on words." It was easy to see how for David verbal communication was unreliable and difficult at best, something apparently common among people with autism (Biklen & Burke, 2006).

David also used sign language in different places, but these expressions tended to be used only in response to teachers or therapists' specific requests to copy them or to complete a "task." For example, during one therapy session, David was required to sign the word "more" before the speech language therapist would give him the next piece to the puzzle he was assembling. To David she said, "What do you need? Tell me with your hands." David then nodded his head and signed "more," and what was interesting was that he then added the sign for "please." "He can sign independently and spontaneously," she told me, "but he's not consistent." It seemed consistency or the lack of it played a dominant part in whether and the degree to which David was able to negotiate shared meaning with others in his life.

David's most common form of communication at home involved a complicated flow of verbal and nonverbal exchanges, where David both vocalized and used his body to express himself, and his communication partner guessed his intended meaning. It was certainly an attempt to negotiate meaning. The following scene illustrates what can best be called a communicative dance:

> When Robin suggested Bobby, Sandy, David, she and I collaborate on assembling a puzzle, David communicated his disinterest by laughing and walking away. When Robin tried to get him back by calling to him, "I need your help, David. Come here" and pulling at his arms, he pinched her. Robin responded, "Don't pinch, don't pinch" and then she initiated a sort of wrestle mixed with massage with David where she patted his stomach and wrapped her legs around his. "Whirrrrr," David said. "Okay" responded Robin to him. "EEEEEeeee. DadadadaUbaua," said David. "Um, hum. Okay," answered Robin.

Robin appeared to be reading David's sounds combined with his movements in an effort to negotiate understanding. David looked as though he was somewhat placated by this interaction until Robin again tried to get David to work on the puzzle. At this point, he stood up, took Robin's hand in his own, and pulled her up.

> "Do you want me to come? Should I come?" Robin asked him. He then led her over to the computer. "Do you want computer?" she asked him. David's vocalizations suddenly changed in form, cadence and tone. "Da da ya ya." They were clear and short and Robin interpreted them to mean "Yes, yes" so she then turned on the computer for him and let him play a game.

This scene illustrates David's success with negotiating meaning. His sustained efforts to communicate his preference for playing a computer game rather than playing with us and the puzzle paid off. Clearly, it took much more time and attention than it would have if David were to have a reliable form of communication readily accessible. However, as this scene and others described in the portrait illustrate, David managed to use what means he had available to successfully communicate with others willing to take the time to listen carefully and who presumed he had something important to say.

*Emerging Themes and Assertions*

Through the analysis of hundreds of pages of field notes, transcriptions, and documents related to David, I began to see patterns in the contexts where he was involved with positive, reciprocal relationships and patterns that reflected habits of interaction based on beliefs and understandings about David. The patterns reveal a sociocultural map of the different types of discourses, or "ways of being in the world," those "connected stretches of language that hang together" (Gee, 1996), surrounding and involving David. In this section, I briefly describe four dominant themes that emerged from my interpretations of David's portrait data.

## CLINICAL AND SPECIAL EDUCATIONAL SERVICES CAN LEAD TO SHRINKING SOCIAL BORDERS

The service systems that were designed to support David in social situations sometimes seemed to work toward further restrictions on his social development opportunities. In other words, the social workers, therapists, medical, and special educational systems constructed patterns of engaging with David that were socially restrictive by limiting his opportunities for contact with nonlabeled peers and naturally occurring social situations.

There are at least three ways that I found that these support systems worked to restrict David's social opportunities. First, their locations were separate and often far away from places where David would more likely engage in natural communication. Second, the language that people used in these professions to do their work put David in a lower social status than most people would be expected to choose for themselves. Third, the patterns of communication these people used when conversing with David tended to be highly directive and task-oriented, something many 10-year-old boys would probably find frustrating and thus unlikely to encourage their genuine communication.

David's weekly team of therapists worked with him in a private building 30 miles from home in a building only used for therapy with children labeled with disabilities. The therapists and medical specialists at the university also observed David and consulted with his parents in a building located a great distance from David's home and his school community. The one exception to this was when a university psychologist observed David for a day in school following the parents' and teacher's request for additional supports.

Although David's IEP stated he was a fourth grader, David remained in the K–2 school after finishing second grade. The IEP justified the segregated setting by explaining that "Students with similar needs are clustered," meaning students who it had been determined needed more supports than others were routinely kept back at the school for younger students until they reached sixth grade. Therefore, even when David was "integrated," he was in classes with children years younger and physically smaller than he. Also, despite the school building's "open school design," where most classrooms were not divided by walls, the special education classrooms were. Even the door to the playground was different than the doors used by other students. Finally, David rode in a separate vehicle from both his "integrated," nonlabeled classmates and from his siblings. The assumption with these segregated placements might have been that they provided David with greater safety, but the message they were giving David and others was that he was not worthy of crossing the social borderland, where he would be able to socialize with nonlabeled children in natural contexts.

In addition to the physical localities of David's support systems being a factor in his social segregation, the language people used who worked in these systems seemed to contribute to his social stigmatization. David was routinely referred to as a "client" by many of the therapists and social service workers. Although their systems might have preferred the word "client" to using their names for confidentiality reasons, the word certainly distances the professional workers from David, and it implies that he was perhaps less of a person than their own titles suggested. The word "client" denotes a person as needy or dependent on others, and its use in these contexts did not seem to promote positive reciprocal relationships. When Jenny, the high school social service worker, said she heard that Robin needed someone to "do David," it seemed to capture this status difference between David and those hired to support him. Jenny and Robin referred to David's classroom as "the severe-profound" class, suggesting that the students who went there became automatic members of a subordinate group of students, students who embody some of the worst sort of characteristics imaginable. I did not hear David's teachers or any of the associates call the classroom by this name, but it is possible that Jenny and Robin's candor revealed a more common parlance regarding how people usually refer to David's classroom. Notably, David's IEP did not describe him as having autism, nor did it provide a name for his classroom; instead it consistently referred to David by name even though his needs were apparently specialized enough to warrant "clustering."

Finally, the third component of the social restrictions put on David by the specialized support systems involved the manner in which people in these systems talked to and interacted with David. The special educational personnel, therapists, and to a lesser extent the social service workers primarily spoke to David rather than conversing with him. I did not see David's general education teacher or either of the specialist teachers address David directly. David's special education teacher and other school support staff often directed David to do something specific, as when one said, "Time to go to the toilet. Put toy away," or he was told to go to his independent work desk, where he faced a wall. When Mrs. Sanlon worked alone with David, she usually asked him display-type questions, where he was expected to respond with a predetermined (typically one-word, single-picture) answer.

Similarly, the therapists told David to follow their directions, which were broken down into simple steps or components, and they used simple sentences when talking to him. Occasionally, I observed the social service workers, the school personnel, and David's mother and sister talk to David with stilted speech and modified sentence structures where the syntax was correct but they might use only a noun and verb. For instance, they might say, "David, play." Apparently this way of talking to David was the technique recommended by the TEACCH method used in Mrs. Sanlon's program. Much of the time, teachers and other adults talked to each other about David in his presence, as was the instance I mentioned earlier, where the associate told me that other children were terrified of David, who was at the time walking with us. Finally, the presence of the associates and their perceived role of managing David's behavior seemed to minimize opportunities for David to develop peer relationships, as was illustrated in the music class scene. Taken together, these ways of conversing and being around and with David dominated the discourse, and they seemed to limit rather than extend his opportunities for communicative possibilities. They provide a picture, or discourse map (Gee, 2005), where organizational structures created to support David appeared to restrict his opportunities to develop positive interactive communication patterns where shared meaning and reciprocal relationships thrive.

## CONSIDERING THE RISKS: "IT'S AN IMPERFECT WORLD."

Although it was clear that David was deeply loved by his family, the social pressures and daily supports David needed began to take their toll on David and his family. General social attitudes and structures that recognize (or accept) only a limited set of behaviors and ways of communicating excluded David and by extension his family from "typical" lifestyles. Robin and Dan talked openly about limitations they endured when they were restricted from accessing regular community activities, such as eating at McDonald's, swimming at water parks, or visiting museums.

David's family struggled with the idea that social conformity provided access to greater social membership. The constant reminders from school and clinical personnel that David was "a problem" made it difficult for David's parents to sustain hope for his future. Robin's own parents repeatedly suggested that she "put him in an institution for the sake of the other children." Although Robin and Dan initially resisted the suggestion, their opposition was waning. They increasingly expressed feeling "exhausted" from cleaning up after him and from trying to get (or keep) David dressed. Robin said that David used to be "very compliant," yet more recently, she said, it was getting tougher to get him to conform, and she feared possible consequences of risking David's safety.

Robin conveyed a sense of tremendous guilt for having to return to work, going so far as to suggest that David's difficulties and subsequent segregation were her fault. She also felt guilty about her responsibilities to her other children. Similarly, Dan blamed himself for not "picking up clues" that apparently David provided him and Dan ignored, which led to David wetting himself while playing on the computer. When Robin wrote to me to inform me of their decision to move David out of their home and into a supervised setting, she described it as "a horrible decision" but said that they felt they could not "risk" the possibility of David getting lost and his siblings feeling guilty about it. Thus, guilt played a part in the risks David's family felt they need to take as part of parenting David. And perhaps without realizing it, in avoiding the risk of losing David, by moving him out of their home, they might have risked relinquishing some of the few possibilities David had in his life for developing positive reciprocal relationships.

In addition to some of the external social pressures that put David's opportunities for reciprocal relationships to develop at risk, David's family and others who interacted with him took on physical and monetary risks. David's family, along with the financial support provided through social services, spent thousands of dollars on specialized therapies and related equipment that may or may not have made a positive difference. The family purchased large quantities of clothing and various shoes in their efforts to try to keep David from undressing. David's school support personnel and his mother told me that David pinched and scratched them. Thus, risks involved with communicating and developing a relationship with David included emotional, physical, and monetary kinds.

It became clear that David also considered the risks involved with social interaction. When I offered him my outstretched hand, I realized that I might be taking a physical risk that he could pinch me; I also feared his rejection, and therefore I took an emotional risk. David, too, I soon realized, took an emotional risk when he reached his hand out to touch me. Each time he made an effort to communicate with others, something that seemed to take great effort on his part, David took tremendous risk that his efforts would not be recognized as meaningful or important enough to warrant the time it might take for the other person to persist in negotiating a shared meaning. Sandy's comment about David's acceptance of her indicated her awareness of the need for both communicative partners to recognize the social, emotional, and possibly even physical risks involved in developing any human relationships, but particularly for David who seemed to struggle for those connections.

## NEGOTIATING POWER: "IT'S HIS WAY TO PROTEST."

A great deal has been written about children's lack of power and need for control, particularly if those children experience communication difficulties (Cazden, 2001; Crossley & McDonald, 1984; Fraser, Lewis, Ding, Kellet, & Robinson, 2005; Graue & Walsh, 1998; Lewis & Lindsay, 2000; Lloyd-Smith & Tarr, 2000). David's difficulty with conventional language and literacy seemed to have reduced his opportunities for developing and exercising control in many areas of his life. At one point, Robin had speculated that David's disrobing might have been "his way to protest." Since David had little if any control over his speech, the integration of his senses (see Amos, Donnellan, Hill, Lapos, Leary, & Lissner-Grant 2005, for information about movement and sensory differences), the places he went, and the people he had access to, it seems worthwhile to seriously consider Robin's comment that controlling what clothes he wore (or did not wear) may have been one of the few situations in his life where he could exercise some control.

Other than exercising control over wearing or not wearing clothes, there were a few other instances I noted when David asserted himself. In situations where David seemed uncomfortable, he changed the environment in ways that did not bother other people. For instance, when there were many people at home and several people talked at the same time, David often covered his ears or he climbed under the desk in the kitchen and made his own sounds, possibly to drown out the competing sounds, as some people with autism have explained (Williams, 1994).

According to the FBA in David's IEP, David's IEP team, which included Mrs. Sanlon, his parents, the school principal, and his SLP, were engaging in a difficult and complex negotiation of power with David. The team decided to continue collecting frequency data on how often David pinched and to make judgments about possible reasons for his actions (the function of the behavior), but it remained unclear whether the team discussed his need for control or whether they planned to discuss in greater depth the reason(s) why David might have wanted to escape.

Despite David's communication difficulties and his limited opportunities to exercise control in his life, especially at school and in therapy, he engaged in ongoing social interactions with a few people when the control of the conversations was shared between them. Many times I heard David's voice interacting with others (but especially members of his family) in the same way that two conventional speakers converse: someone talked, then David took his turn and vocalized something, and then the first person interpreted what David said and added his or her own response. Additionally, I observed David and others use nonverbal forms of communication, such as signs, gestures, both idiosyncratic and more conventional movements, as well as AAC forms of communication (e.g., pictures, the Dynavox) to negotiate meaning and understanding. These were clearly interactive, co-constructed communicative exchanges that illustrate Bakhtin's (1984) description of the "dialogic fabric of human life." In these situations, David was offered (and he accepted) the chance to engage in constructing shared meaning.

Cazden (2001) studied the opportunities students were provided to speak in classroom contexts. She wrote, "The most important asymmetry in the rights and obligations of teachers and students is over control of the right to speak" (p. 82). Cazden's idea of *speaking rights*, "the ways by which students get the right to talk—to be legitimate speakers," is a useful idea for discussing David's communication. It suggests that David should have had the right to speak, or in his case to use whatever means he might have to communicate, to contribute his thoughts and feelings to others at school (and, arguably, in other contexts as well). The other part of speaking rights, Cazden asserted, is *listening responsibilities*, where teachers (and others) listen and respond to students' voices. Thus, Cazden suggested that teachers (and researchers) pay attention to the ways in which teachers talk to and listen to their students (or participants). Therefore, I looked for times and ways in which people had expectations for David to "speak" and how they listened to what David was "saying."

Few people talked directly to David and those who did sometimes used an altered cadence (somewhat stilted), a higher pitch, and/or shortened sentences. The adults in David's special education classroom described students as "good" if the children immediately complied with verbal directives or if they were quietly and independently working; students were described as "bad" if they got up from their desks or made vocalizations. Therefore, like his classmates in the special education classroom, David was generally discouraged from talking. Furthermore, the teachers in David's "integrated" classrooms did not address him directly nor did they ask him to contribute to class discussions.

Throughout my visits with David, I noticed how some people gave voice to their interpretations of David's vocalizations and behaviors as a way of providing David with speaking rights and as a way of listening to him: when David put his fingers in his ears and Mrs. Sanlon said to him, "You're mad. What's ya mad about? You want me to go?"; when David walked in the hallway with Terry and squealed "Ee aa ooa" and Terry said to a passing adult, "He's angry"; and finally when Sandy, the respite worker, said that much of what David did was easily interpreted, such as the time she took out the Dynavox and asked him what he wanted and he pressed the "shut down" button and shoved it away. David's family seemed to most often interpret and revoice David's actions and sounds. The best example was Robin's revoicing David's happiness by saying, "Oh, I'm so excited! Look at me!" The voiced interpretations provided David with a voice that might not otherwise be part of the conversation, thus confirming David's right to participate in the social environments where he lived. It is important to note that the content of the interpretations might well be different from what David intended, but if indeed Robin was correct in her interpretation, she recognized David's efforts to call attention to himself and to seek acknowledgment.

*David's Emerging Literacy as a Possible Avenue into Social Relationships*

David showed an interest in symbol systems, and sometimes that interest allowed him to share experiences with and occasionally interact with his nondisabled classmates. According to David's father, David had "always been very good at shapes." He seemed drawn to shapes, and he demonstrated an understanding of how the orientation of certain shapes express meaning when he read and signed a story on the computer with his teacher. Several people told me that David excelled in assembling puzzles, some with as many as 100 pieces. His occupational therapist indicated that David was successful with creating letters. He used pictures and words to read and interact with people at school and home.

David also showed an interest in books. "Ever since he was little," Robin explained, "he would pick out books at the library." David's K–1 teacher wrote how David used to like to sit with an older student who came to him and read books to him. It was common to find David looking through books, front to back, pausing long enough to read each page. I observed him reading books while using the toilet, sitting on the floor in front of the glass doors, in the therapist's waiting room, and at the library. David's home was filled with books, and David had ready access to them. One day when I visited him, he was looking through stacks of books from the bookshelves in the hallway outside his bedroom. David's younger brother, Bobby, showed a similar love of books when he pulled nearly 20 books from his backpack, stacking them on the floor after reading aloud each book's title.

David's mother and teacher agree that David understands the meaning of several words. Early in the study, Robin described her son as literate; "David is a reader," she told me. David's IEP stated that he "receptively reads seventy words." David regularly read the combined picture–word schedules at home, therapy, and school. For years, David used a picture exchange communication system where he traded palm-sized black and white drawings with communication partners in order to get tangibles or access to an activity. He also read and negotiated meaning using multiple levels of picture–word combinations in the Dynavox communication system. Additionally, David demonstrated both literacy skills and computer skills when using computers at home and at school. Many of these text-related systems seemed to provide David with opportunities for engaging in social dialogue.

Thus, in addition to his emerging literacy in reading and writing, David showed some skills in what Gallas (2003) called "sociocultural literacy." He "read" many nonverbal social communication signs. For instance, when his family began to pack up their camping supplies, Robin thought he took off his clothes because he did not want to leave. David engaged in taking turns with his mother and others who conversed with him. After nodding his head to answer Jenny's question about going to the library, David walked to the door and slipped on his shoes. David also seemed to accurately "read" when he could move closer to the little girl in his music class. I observed him sharing control of the mouse and engaging in related conversations with others while he was on the computer. Finally, David's early childhood teacher had explained how David enjoyed sharing books with a young guest reader who he then befriended. The fourth and final theme that emerged from David's portrait (his emerging literacy) seemed to provide David with an opportunity to develop shared understanding and reciprocal relationships where otherwise few other opportunities existed in a life dominated by socially restrictive programs and services.

In conclusion, the communicative dance in which David and certain people (his family members, a few service workers, and on occasion his special education teacher) in his life engaged represents a larger, changing social discourse (Gee, 1999) where nonconventional communicators are sometimes viewed positively and thus from a different cultural model than the negative dominant model in current special education and social service systems (Bogdan & Taylor, 1987; Ferguson, Ferguson, & Taylor, 1992; Kliewer & Biklen, 2007). By offering David an opportunity to actively participate in meaningful conversations in whatever way he was able, these people shared the power of voiced thoughts. When David accepted (or demanded) the opportunity to communicate, he exercised his right to be heard as well as creating the possibility for developing reciprocal relationships. By contrast, when David was not allowed access to meaningful and motivating activities, when he was rarely able to exercise any control over his life, or when he was discouraged from vocalizing or acting out his thoughts and feelings, he might have been resorting to whatever means he had available to take some control, for instance, by taking off his clothing.

Unfortunately, only a few people in David's life seemed to be able to permeate the more dominant social discourse, where disability defines a person and restricted his social world. These few people, along with David, were actively re-creating their "storylines" (Gee, 1999) of local understanding (Kliewer & Biklen, 2007), where they sometimes chose to accept the social, emotional, and physical risks in order to engage in positive reciprocal relationships. The troublesome aspect of David's story was that these few people began to question their own ability to continue working with David, and so David's efforts to take control might have led to even less control over his life, as he moves into a residential care home.

# CHAPTER 3

# Katie's Portrait

FIGURE 5.  *Katie's self-portrait.*

## MEETING KATIE: THE THEATRICAL COMMUNITY
## STRUGGLES WITH ACCEPTING KATIE

I had known Katie for over a year when she asked me to attend her rehearsal for the high school's theatrical performance of *High School Musical.* Like her parents and older brother, Katie had been involved in the performing arts throughout her life. I had seen her perform in *Beauty and the Beast* the previous year. During one of my first visits with Katie as part of this study, we met at a coffee shop, where she sat beside me at my computer while we took turns typing a list of topics and details about her for what we called her "biography story" (this study). Here is an excerpt:

> Singing is what I do. When I was a little girl I went to church with my mom and I was singing. Plays. *Cinderella*. I threw up because I had stage fright—a long time ago—chorus. After that I was in *Grease* where I wore a black shirt, a red scarf and a polka dot poodle skirt. When I was in that play I had really short hair. *Godspell*. I was a totem; we had to greet each other. I raised my arms up over our heads. We hugged each other. I was hugging [a girl]. I had Math class with her last year at school. Every day last year whenever I saw her, she told me I had to practice [singing and signing the song] "Day by Day." She got annoyed. When I was a kid, I was in *Alice in Wonderland*, probably in Elementary School.

Clearly, Katie identified herself as a performer, a singer; another time she said, "I'm a pop diva." The performing arts provided Katie with a context where she could potentially emerge as a competent and contributing member.

Katie's participation in the school play had been encouraged by her father, the high school's music director, something Katie said was "embarrassing." Although Katie's father transferred to another school during the summer and therefore was no longer part of her school's theatrical performances, Katie auditioned and secured a part in the annual musical: *High School Musical*. I was familiar with the plot of the story because Katie owned a DVD copy of the Disney movie, and as a result of her repeated viewings of the video, she could recite scenes verbatim. Once she had me sit in her backyard and watch while she performed both parts of an entire scene from the play.

The theme of the play was about accepting nonconformity. It was one of Katie's favorite scripts. She often referred to herself as Gabriella, the main female character who struggled to find acceptance in a new high school. Gabriella is extremely smart, and the play follows her efforts to break free from the stereotype that puts her in with the "brainiac" crowd (Disney Enterprises, 2006, p. 68). The play's song "Stick to the Status Quo" (Lawrence & Greenberg, 2005) captures the tension of students being discouraged from breaking the social grouping norms because it is "dangerous" (Disney Enterprises, 2006, p. 71). But in the end, the students decide it is all right to "start something new" (Disney Enterprises, 2006, p. 112), to blur the social barriers between traditionally segregated groups.

When I arrived at Katie's rehearsal for the show, I found the cast practicing the choreography to the song "Together." This comes at the end of the play, when the high school had become "a different place, where everybody could follow the beat of their own drummer, and other people would cheer them on . . . a place where people could have fun . . . together" (Disney Enterprises, 2006, p.138). More than 50 teenagers, many donned in holey jeans and tie-dyed t-shirts, followed the directions of the choreographer.

While the song played, the students were supposed to sing along and dance, some-what informally but together. Suddenly the music director stopped the CD player and yelled, "Please make an effort not to have anyone dancing alone. It's completely against what you're singing about." Apparently, she found it "ironic" that Katie was dancing in the front row mostly by herself. "Pay attention. No loners now," the music director added before replaying the song and resuming the rehearsal.

I recalled the man from Hutton who said "We're unaccepting of differences." In the high school's lunchroom, I witnessed other students' struggle to accept Katie. Katie was making an effort to break out of the socially constructed and stigmatizing disability world (Taylor, 2000). But she was slowly being recognized by others around her (like the music director), and she was now being legitimized through her membership in the theatrical community, or "family," as one student reporter had called the cast in a recent school newspaper article.

The scene above illustrates how efforts to contest social borders do not come easily. Despite the fact that throughout Katie's school there were posters touting the virtues of acceptance, and the large exterior school billboard said "Embrace our differences," Katie's differences stigmatized her to the point that no one in the play rehearsal danced with her. One of Katie's teachers put it this way: "The kids show her kindness, but they aren't her friends." Katie was indeed a cast member, but I questioned the nature of that membership.

## KATIE'S SOCIAL WORLDS: THE EFFORT TO FIND A VALUED PLACE

*Katie and Schooling: Between Worlds or "No World"?*

Washington High has over 1,500 students in grades 9 through 12. The special education coordinator explained that the school serves more than 120 students "on IEPs," meaning those students who are identified as having disabilities, such as Katie. The coordinator noted, "There is another program for students considered to be severe/profound which is located at the other public high school." Then she added, "We used to be more seg-regated. . . . I'm for inclusion, like not all BD kids [meaning students with the diagnosis of behavioral disorder] in one room, but if you put a student in a General Education room with 30 other students, they just won't learn . . . it doesn't rub off. The students have special needs which are not to be ignored." Her explanation suggested a tension in the school regarding the role of special education. In order to serve (not ignore) students like Katie, the teacher seemed to believe, special education should provide specialized curricula in separate environments from their unlabeled peers instead of placing them in an inclusive setting where "they just won't learn."

Katie was an 18-year-old senior when I observed her rehearsal for *High School Musical.* Earlier in the year, on another occasion when we sat together at a coffee shop, she typed on my laptop: "I take Basic English." Then she turned to me and said, "I sit by my friends and someone I do not know." I was unsure how to interpret this last comment. Katie often referred to some classmates as "friends," and she was quick to introduce me to several of them. She is good at remembering names, so I was never able to sort out whether the person she sat next to was new, thus explaining her reference to "someone I do not know," or whether she and this particular classmate just chose not to acquaint themselves with one another.

For the next several minutes, Katie typed a list of her classes, including speech, math, "Business training where we do keyboarding," choir, senior seminar, and "after English I have Photography." Here Katie added verbally, "This is my first time to take [photography]. I took it because I wanted to take different classes, to be with different people. I want to be different." Previously, Katie had referred to the students in her life skills[1] classes (most of whom also had trisomy 21) as being "normal." In light of this, her comment about wanting to be "different" suggested a desire to be different from the students with whom she had predominantly been educated and socialized, different from the role the school had assigned her.

It was comments like "I want to be different" that exemplified what I view as Katie's struggle with socially constructed borders between two worlds: One world was where students took life skills classes, and the other, "different," world was where students took classes like speech and photography. She was indicating an awareness of these two separate worlds, one of which she seemed to want to exit. This conversation was one of many that led me to think of Katie as someone who was willing to take risks by asserting herself and seeking recognition for her individuality.

During Katie's junior year, her mother, Carol, observed Katie in life skills classes. In one class, Katie was expected to sweep up dirt that a teacher had put on the floor. Sweeping was a task that had been analyzed and broken down into its component parts in the form of a checklist. Katie and the other students were told to follow the steps in the correct order; transgressions meant the students had to start over from the beginning. Another task was cleaning windows. Subsequently, Carol and her husband, Jim, pushed for a change in their daughter's educational program to what they considered to be more interesting and challenging. They typed up a two-page document outlining their "Thoughts regarding Katie's educational programming" and gave it to the school personnel. In the document, they asserted that Katie was spending "less than 15% of her time in successful academic pursuits." They explained their concern for the school's "overemphasis" and "misinterpretation" of Katie's "misbehaviors," their desire for the

---

[1] According to the district Web site, "life skills" means "mental disability." These terms are presented as synonymous and defined as "Significantly subaverage general intellectual functioning existing concurrently with deficits in adaptive behavior and manifested during the developmental period that adversely affects an individual's educational performance." In practice, the term "life skills" is used to describe an educational program where students are taught skills determined necessary for functioning in daily life.

school to discontinue the tabulation and charting of these behaviors and to increase her access to the general education curriculum.

Following several meetings between Katie's parents and her teachers, a novel combination of classes (those Katie listed above) was offered to Katie. Her new IEP indicated a near 50–50 split in her time between special and general education classes with adult assistance (i.e., from a paraprofessional or associate); this was something Carol said had not previously been done at Washington for students considered to have moderate disabilities. I observed Katie in this new schedule, where she actively participated in discussions about current political and social issues and researched and presented reports and speeches alongside her classmates without obvious problems.

Katie said she enjoyed her new schedule despite the fact that, according to Carol, Katie spent hours doing homework every night and several of her teachers expressed frustration with Katie's "distracted" and "inappropriate behaviors" in their monthly progress reports. For example, Katie had to "redo" an assignment for Foods II because she got only 9.5 out of 70. She had answered the first 11 questions correctly. Question 12 was, "Explain the problem with the typical American consumption of protein," to which Katie answered "Is this supposed to be a trick question?" Her answers to Questions 13 and 14 were "See #12." Question 63 was, "Summarize in your own words what you have learned about the tenderness of meat and poultry," to which Katie answered, "I would like to dance on the tops of tables in high heels." Carol explained that those who knew Katie would understand that her answer to Question 63 was a line from the Broadway show *Rent*. Carol thought it was a clear indication that Katie was confused or bored with the assignment, rather than an accurate display of Katie's content knowledge or an example of an "inappropriate behavior."

Carol was irritated with the school rather than with her daughter. She described Katie's new program as just another "box"—more challenging but still "mostly within special education." Her use of the metaphor of a "box" to describe special education reiterated the teacher's view in a dichotomous relationship between two different programs. The separate programming "boxes" create an image where clearly defined lines exist and something (students) could be placed inside (life skills/special education classes) and the lids could be closed (restricted borders). The box metaphor suggests that special education is a world unto itself with uncontestable borders between it and the world of general education. Katie's efforts to be different, to seek membership in the world of general education, did not seem to be entirely working.

Katie's display of her imagination might have allowed her greater acceptance in the world outside her life skills classes except for the unusual nature in which she sometimes used it, thus again leaving her in a sort of limbo between two worlds. One of Katie's teachers told me how much she enjoyed Katie, but she thought that Katie's imagination interfered with Katie's ability to develop peer relationships, indicating that although she attributed value to Katie's imagination, she blamed Katie for lack of self-regulation. She

explained how Katie sometimes adopted other people's names as her own. "One week she
became someone from a movie. She called herself by the actress's name and even wrote
it on her papers. Then she pretended to be a girl from another class," which apparently
bothered the girl. "As adults we know it as imagination," the teacher said, "but the kids
don't see it that way." It seemed that Katie's imagination was problematic in the academic
venue, in contrast to the theatrical community, which potentially offered Katie a social
context where her imagination was valued and viewed as contributing to her membership.

Like her imagination, Katie's somewhat unconventional use of language and literacy
sometimes appeared to clash with the "different" world where she sought membership.
Katie sometimes sends cards or letters to schoolmates, but according to Carol, Katie
does not receive phone calls or letters in return. Two years ago Katie's efforts to befriend
another member of the school play were initially reciprocated, but when she began to
write the girl letters expressing her affection, the girl's mother said that her daughter
became uncomfortable. "It became inappropriate," the mother told me on the phone;
so the girl's mother sought and gained the school's assistance with an intervention that
effectively ended the relationship between the girls. Katie later told me she thought the
girl's mother had "gotten in the way," and she thought if she could just talk directly with
the girl, they could work it out.

Katie's more recent effort to develop a friendship with a sophomore also nearly ended
when a teacher approached the girl to ask whether she felt comfortable with Katie. The
girl, whom I will call Cindy, seemed to genuinely enjoy Katie, talking at length with her
on the phone on at least one occasion when Katie called her to wish her a happy 16th
birthday. Cindy told her mother that she thought the teacher's comment was meant for
her "to back off of her relationship with Katie." "Until then," according to Cindy's
mom, "she hadn't thought there was anything 'wrong'; she knew what Katie meant" when
Katie wrote her a letter saying "I want you and you want me."[2] Unstated, but understood
by people who know Katie well, was that Katie meant she wanted to share in a friendship.
She often signs her letters "Love, Katie" or "Always be mine."

When Katie's parents learned about the misunderstanding, they were upset enough
that Jim wrote the teacher: "I do want Katie to continue learning about appropriate communication. . . . However, you may have damaged the one true friendship Katie has managed to develop at Washington." Jim's comments suggest he thought the teacher acted as
a social barrier, as some sort of gatekeeper to maintain the border between the students
of the special education world and those of the general education world.

Carol explained how the apparent separation between these two worlds or "boxes"
was less obvious in Katie's early schooling. However, she noticed Katie's full member-

---

[2] I did not seek an interview with Cindy because it seemed her relationship with Katie was already under too
much scrutiny, and I did not want to jeopardize it. But this relationship certainly appeared to illustrate a
positive reciprocal relationship.

ship in general education beginning to erode during second grade. She thought Katie's teacher did not hold values showing Katie and her classmates the importance of Katie's membership. "Values people have—they can't turn them on all of a sudden because they have a child in their room with special needs." Carol described Katie's role in the room as a visitor. "Unless she's there [regularly], the more she seems like she's just visiting. She's just there until she's got to go back [to a special education classroom]." Carol's sentiments echo Jim's comment about the importance of teachers' perceptions and expectations and how they sometimes seem to interfere with Katie's efforts to be "different," to break free from stigmatizing stereotypes.

Despite Katie's diversity of social circles, which now included more general education classes in addition to her extracurricular activities, she continued to struggle for reciprocity in interpersonal relationships. Carol said that Katie expressed concern that neither the girls in her old life skills classes nor those in her new classes and in the play seemed to want to be friends. "She wishes they [i.e., her nonlabeled peers] would pay attention to her." Carol continued: "So it's like she's in no, [pause] not in any world right now. . . . She goes to music rehearsal. She loves that. And she talks about the kids and the leads and she's really excited about that. But there's no reciprocation." Katie's apparent struggle with finding a place, or in Carol's words, "any world" where she belonged, is illustrative of Anzaldua's (1999) "borderlands."

It seems that Katie and one or two other high school students had attempted to disrupt the externally determined, unnatural social borders between special and general education program structures. Their friendships offered an alternative world to the various "boxes" Carol mentioned. Their efforts might be described as similar to Giroux's (1992) "*border crossings,* in which voice develops through a physical and intellectual journey beyond boundaries of classroom, of culture, of home and school learning" (as quoted in MacBeath, 2006, p. 195).

Members of the high school theater "family" appeared to be in the midst of living out the theme of the play, where they contested the status quo social boundaries to a greater or lesser extent. The girls' actions took on an element of risk when some adults suggested social impropriety. In the case of the first relationship, Katie told me she thought her friend's mother had gotten in the way. Carol thought the friendship had dissolved due to a misunderstanding of Katie's expressed affection, when she wrote letters and used the word "love." In the second friendship, the teacher who had approached Cindy inadvertently implied that she should "back off." In both instances, adults seemed to have interfered with budding relationships, thus reinforcing the idea of social borders.

*Support Services and Katie: Another Struggle to Be "Appropriate"*

I first met Katie during a carpooling ride to the university where Carol and I took a class together. Katie and I shared the backseat of her mother's sedan while another graduate student sat in the front seat with Carol. "This is me dressed up for prom," Katie explained, showing me the first of many photographs she held in her hand. Katie leaned in close to me, her teenage cheeks aglow with pride as she caught my eyes glancing back and forth between the formally dressed young woman in the photograph and the girl in a t-shirt, jeans, and pink tennis shoes who was sitting beside me.

Later I learned that Katie had not joined her classmates at prom that year. Instead, her mother dropped her off at Sue's college dormitory apartment, where a few of Sue's friends were gathering specifically to celebrate prom with Katie. Sue and Katie became friends when Sue began joining Katie out in the community as part of the social service program supported by the MR waiver.[3] Although Sue had since moved on from being a community support worker, she continued her contact with Katie, which led her to offer Katie an alternative prom experience. So, indirectly, the support service program had indeed provided Katie with a social experience similar to her nondisabled peers, but the difference—a somewhat unnatural gathering—suggested that Katie experienced social exclusion and segregation in settings outside the academic arena. In other words, attending the prom with a date connotes a particular social status that Katie apparently did not have.[4]

The social service system is designed to support Katie's daily life experiences in her community, yet her parents expressed conflicted feelings about the program. One evening Carol described a parent-led meeting she and Jim attended when Katie was a toddler:

> I remember thinking, "We don't really need to be here. I don't feel like we need to come to a meeting where there are all these kids with special needs running around. I just don't"—and it seemed to me like other parents were just all concerned about things. And I thought to myself, "Should I be concerned about those things? I'm not concerned about those things. Am I missing something?" And then I remember hearing about the [MR] waiver program and thinking "Should we do that? I don't think we need that. Why should we deserve that? Does Katie need that? I don't know."

---

[3] The Department of Human Services provides a variety of services to individuals who meet certain eligibility criteria for the MR waiver. One criterion is determination of mental retardation by a licensed psychologist. The services include "respite" and "supported community living [CSL]." Accordingly, "respite care services are services" that provide "temporary relief to the usual caregiver [enabling] the consumer to remain in the consumer's current living situation" (retrieved from www.dhs.state.ia.us/docs/MRPacket. doc). Guidelines suggest that respite care or CSL be provided "in the consumer's home, another family's home, camps, [or] organized community programs [such as] YMCA, recreation centers," and so forth, "to assist the consumer with daily living needs."

[4] The following year Katie joined a young man from the life skills program for prom. They went out to dinner at a restaurant while their mothers sat at a table nearby, but the couple were then dropped off at the general high school prom.

Carol and Jim did not identify themselves as members of the larger social system network designed to support people with disabilities and their families. Not until Katie was 15 did they include Katie (and thus themselves) in the MR waiver program. "It was just kind of weird that we were kind of lumped into this [group or program]," Carol said. "We qualify for respite because we have a daughter who has Down syndrome and that's just an automatic respite-getter," but she did not feel that they needed respite from their daughter. Instead, Carol and Jim indicated that the only reason they enrolled Katie in the program was to insure benefits for her after her 18th birthday.

Katie never talked to me about her feelings regarding support services per se, but I noticed differences between the content and quantity of her conversations when she was with her social service worker, or "trainer," as she was called, and in other contexts with other people. Katie informed me that she usually went with her "trainer," Mary, to the library where Katie volunteered, to the ice cream shop, or to the YMCA, where I joined them one late afternoon. Mary brought a large bag filled with games, cards, Chinese checkers, worksheet books, and other materials including paper and markers, which she set on a table in the entrance to the Y. The bag's contents and the accompanying scene reminded me of vocational rehabilitation programs I had observed decades earlier.

Katie was not talking, something I found unusual, until Mary went to the bathroom. Katie was instructing me in the rules of Old Maid when we were joined by a middle-school-age girl and her "trainer." Shortly thereafter a third social service worker and her male "client" also joined us. The three "trainers" referred to the girls and the boy as their "clients" while they talked to each other about these youths, their schedules, and training requirements for keeping their jobs. Occasionally the women interrupted our card game to remind the girls to "be nice." The boy stood by the window and seemed to watch people come and go. His worker told me "He's autistic," as though she was explaining to me why he was not expected to converse or play with the other kids.

Earlier, Katie and Mary and I had sat in a booth at an ice cream shop while Mary told me how Katie needed to work on saying "please" and "thank you." I had noticed that the shop worker addressed Mary rather than Katie when Katie ordered a kid's meal. Like she had at the Y, Mary talked about Katie in her presence in ways I felt were patronizing. On another occasion, Mary told me that Katie "was not social," but my observations of Katie at home, in school, and in other places when she was not with other labeled people or their trainers suggested otherwise. One possible unintended consequence of systematizing social support systems for Katie was that it disempowered her in social circumstances. The language of the social service system (e.g., "trainer") emphasized this power issue, where Katie was placed in a position of being socially trained or conditioned to act a certain way ("nice" or "appropriate") and to play certain (childlike) games in certain contexts (at the YMCA with other "clients"). Instead of Mary's interpretation that Katie was "not social," Katie might have been choosing not to participate in the social contexts offered to her through the social service agency.

The idea that Katie's membership in the social service system meant a less-than-respectable social status was reinforced nearly a year later when I joined Katie at a Christmas party for "clients" of the social service system and their families. After dinner, the lights dimmed and a DJ began playing music, and Katie went out onto the dance floor and remained there until the party ended. Just before Katie left us at the table, Mary reminded her to "dance appropriately." While I danced with whoever was willing to join me (Katie avoided me most of the time), I noticed Mary and a few other social service workers standing at the edges of the dance floor watching. One social service worker warned me, "You've got to keep an eye on them," suggesting he thought the girls were promiscuous, or at least less than "appropriate."

Again, at the end of the party, Katie's independence and freedom to form her own relationships was scrutinized in unnatural ways. After most of the people had cleared the dance floor, Katie and a young man named Austin stood facing each other in what might have otherwise been a romantic moment. With Mary standing a few yards away watching, Katie handed Austin a card she had bought for him. Katie and Austin and the other "clients," some of whom were over 21 years of age, were watched so closely and at times talked about in their presence that their membership in the social support system seemed to equate to a lowered status that effectively reduced their power and opportunities for forming reciprocal relationships. Additionally, the language used in the social service system seemed to contribute to reinforcing negative stereotypes, and thus perhaps it was the language (e.g., "respite") as much as the programming practices that made Carol question her decision to apply for their services.

## KATIE'S HOME LIFE: AN UNCERTAIN FUTURE

In the nearly 20 years since Katie's birth, her parents have been very involved with Katie's medical, social, and educational life. Jim and Carol described being overwhelmed when they received Katie's diagnosis of trisomy 21 and experiencing her related physical complications. Carol said she remembered when Katie came home from the hospital: "All of a sudden our house was full of people." There were speech and physical therapists, social workers, and others who entered their home and their lives to provide support. This support was met by Jim and Carol with mixed feelings and results.

Jim said that his role in Katie's life as the "tough love giver" began in her first days of life when he had to hit his daughter's back with a small, soft, hammer-like tool to keep fluid from collecting in her lungs. "Katie's got a tough life ahead of her," he said when describing Katie's recurring health issues. With great empathy he explained Katie's "bona fide, justifiable fear of toileting. Can you imagine, that primary bodily function being a fearful effort?" He seemed exasperated by their repeated efforts to get help for Katie from the medical experts.

Similarly, Carol expressed her frustration with what she viewed as arbitrary eligibility requirements for some support services in contrast to eligibility requirements for other services:

> [Katie] didn't get speech therapy until 1st or 2nd grade. I think it was 2nd grade, when she—we finally had the argument that her—because she was learning to write. She was writing like she was talking. She was putting down the wrong letters. But up until then that the argument was she cannot have speech because her language development age is higher than her overall developmental age. And until her developmental age is beyond her linguistic or whatever age, then she does not qualify . . . we kept asking for it . . . Speech teachers say "She's really capped out. She's—she articulates as good as she's going to. No matter how much longer we spend on this, she still says her [letter] *r*s the same way.

More recently Katie's parents had been concerned with preparing her for greater independence in an uncertain future. As I mentioned previously, they advocated for more rigorous educational programming, and they were beginning to discuss Katie's possible living arrangements outside their home following her high school graduation. However, they were somewhat anxious about Katie's sexual development and her management of money. Carol said that she and Katie had talked with a doctor about birth control, but Carol indicated Jim was leaning more toward having Katie surgically sterilized. Carol described how when Katie was told her school lunch account was running low, Katie took her parents' checkbook and wrote the school a $50 check. The same day she wrote a check and mailed it to a company for graduation announcements. Although they might have viewed Katie's assertiveness and independence as admirable, Carol and Jim feared that Katie could mistakenly write a much larger check, so they hid their checkbook and made money management a goal for the social service program.

Regarding Katie's social life, her parents described a younger Katie as one who was always invited to parties and who played with her brother and other children in their neighborhood. Jim said that the children who lived next door used to come to their house and ask him to play the guitar or they would help him with landscaping projects, providing Katie with social contact with peers. As Katie got older, she became involved in theater and sports after school, or she stayed at school and rode home with her father.

Because her parents' schedules had changed in her fifth year of high school, Katie began taking the bus (for students in special education), and she stayed home alone for increasingly longer periods of time. For Katie, this meant less access to social opportunities with her nondisabled peers but also increased independence. During my after-school visits, she moved about her house with confidence, making us strawberry smoothies and sandwiches. She also cleaned her second-floor bedroom, where she enjoyed playing music on her drum set, on her guitar, or on her CD player.

Katie's 18th birthday party illustrates some of the complexities involved in her home life and social relationships. Upon each guest's arrival, Katie skipped to the dining room and reemerged with a brightly colored lei that she gently placed over the guest's head. For the first hour, Katie danced barefooted to hula music, sometimes alone and other times with others she had recruited to join her. About 20 people attended, including her father, mother, and older brother, who was home from college. Some of Katie's aunts surprised her by driving several hours to attend. A family Katie and her family had befriended through their church also came, along with the owner of the coffee shop where Katie and her mother frequently spent their time. Mary the social service worker was there with her daughter. I was there, as were a few other friends with their families. None of Katie's classmates came, but later Austin arrived and he and Katie spent some alone time swinging on the front porch.

One of the adults at the party asked Carol, "Are any of Katie's friends coming?" Carol later wrote me an e-mail in which she questioned the underlying meaning of the question. "This has really bothered me and I have thought about it a lot since the party." She continued:

> I think Katie sees all of the people that were there as her friends and—or relatives. Katie and I created the guest list together, and besides one person I suggested she add, she came up with all of the names. . . . I am beginning to think more and more that this age difference between her and the others with whom she socializes does not matter to Katie nearly as much as it concerns me . . . and it is concerning me less as I see her happy and accepted by other adults who she makes happy and who love her.

Carol's comment illustrates the impact of externally defined social constructions of what constitutes "appropriate" relationships. "If Lolly is her best friend, maybe that's okay, even though Lolly is 45 [years old]," Carol said, admitting, "I'm just putting on this superficial thing, you know, that she should have friends her own age."

Carol also questioned her assumptions about Katie's future home life. "I used to think that she needed to be by people 'like her.'" Carol said she had originally envisioned Katie moving into a group home, a duplex next door, or a supervised apartment. "Now I'm not so sure that's necessary . . . I'm still in transition." She continued, "The group home is out." It seemed that Carol was struggling with divergent expectations for her daughter's future, much like Katie herself struggled with the social restrictions imposed on her in educational environments.

Katie's home life, school life, and time spent in the community with (and without) social services intersect, but how Katie fit within each of these contexts is unclear. At times, such as at her party, she appeared confident, happy, and in control of the social interaction. Yet some of her opportunities (or meaningful reasons) for participation in the larger social network seemed restricted by the very systems (e.g., special education, social services) designed to support her in these contexts. Katie's father explained how her life is micromanaged by adults whose job it is to keep a watch on her. He made the point that it would be difficult to learn self-control if one is not given the opportunities to make mistakes.

Katie's future home and social life seemed similarly vague. Carol said, "I want her to choose what she wants to do," but she and Jim decided it would be best for Katie to stay in high school for another year in order to earn a regular diploma. Carol expressed hope that the school personnel would develop relationships with Katie where they would talk to her, "not down to her." She wished they would "set an expectation that [Katie] is a member of the class, a member of the community." Her comments highlight what it means to be taken seriously as an individual and to become a valued member in a school or community environment.

In summary, during the time when I studied Katie and her relationships, I saw her social circles change. She was breaking away from relationships within what could be thought of as the disability world, but she was not fully included in the world where she might socialize if she did not have a disability. Instead, her mother suggested during one of our last conversations, "Katie is part of a third world." She thought Katie was in effect creating a new world, one where she was fully functional and appeared to be accepted. Carol suggested that that "third world" existed in a moment of time in her home on Katie's 18th birthday and she seemed to hope it would find a place in her daughter's future. Carol's rebuff of the group home indicated a rejection of the traditional trajectory for people with trisomy 21 in Hutton.

In her senior year, Katie was no longer part of the life skills program, nor was she taking part in the teacher-directed social skills curriculum. She was not escorted by an adult associate like she had been for much of her educational career. Although she continued to enjoy participating in the world of her peers who were also labeled with a disability—she liked dancing at the Goodwill Christmas party, participating in Special Olympics, and attending a weekend camp for youth with disabilities—she also seemed to reject that world by taking general education electives and remedial-type classes geared for students considered to have normal intelligence, where Katie sought friendships with students who she thought were "different."

## WAYS OF KNOWING KATIE

There were many people involved in Katie's life who I thought contributed to her social development and sense of self, but I elected to focus on a few relationships. The first two relationships I discuss include Katie's mother and father. Lolly, the third person on whom I focus in this section, offers insight into her positive reciprocal relationship with

Katie. Then I describe some of the nuances of my own relationship that developed with Katie during the course of this study. Finally, Katie speaks for herself. In this last section, I present several pieces of Katie's own words and use of symbolic communication.

## KATIE AND CAROL: "I CAN'T IMAGINE LIFE WITHOUT HER."

Carol thinks deeply about her relationship with Katie, and she readily acknowledges its complexity. She expressed empathy for and mutual understanding with her daughter, who she frequently described as having a wonderful sense of humor. "I can't imagine life without her," Carol declared after a busy week filled with meetings and paperwork as part of Katie's transition into adulthood. "It seems like I am transitioning from strictly a mother role to that of a friend as well. She teaches me so much about how to live in the present."

In her parent role, Carol seemed to struggle with society's stereotypical and stigmatizing interpretation of Katie. In the larger world, trisomy 21 (Becker, 1963; Taylor, 2000) dominated how Katie was known—she was often primarily defined by her status as disabled or something other than fully human. This status clashed with Carol's own intimate local knowledge of her daughter. Carol described her constant uncertainty about how much of what Katie does "is her personality versus how much is her disability." As an example, she described a situation where Katie did not respond to something Carol had said to her. Carol presumed that Katie must not have heard her because of an ear infection, but Jim thought Katie was just ignoring her mother.

On the one hand, Carol celebrated Katie's idiosyncrasies and sometimes viewed them as strengths, like Katie's sense of humor, her unabashed freedom with dancing, and her ability to break out into song to cheer up her mother. On the other hand, Carol wanted Katie to dress according to social norms, like when she pleaded with her daughter "not to wear socks with sandals 'cause it's dorky." Carol pushed for Katie to be included in more general education classes, but she also supported Katie's participation in Special Olympics and camps for children with disabilities. She recognizes Katie's intelligence, her literacy and performance skills, and her developing maturity; however, she grappled with how to talk to her daughter about issues of sexuality and what it means in society to have trisomy 21.

As friends, Carol and Katie enjoy each other's company and humor. They routinely sit side by side at the coffee shop or on their porch swing, Carol working on her laptop and Katie watching a DVD. They frequent Broadway musicals and movies. Carol had begun to write a play for Katie. One summer afternoon while sitting with me at her kitchen table, Carol shared a story that made her cry. Katie had been walking in and out of the kitchen, talking and singing into the voice recorder, then listening back to it. Upon seeing her mother's eyes well up, Katie stopped, turned to her, and began singing, "I've got sunshine on a cloudy day." Katie's recognition of her mother's sorrow and her effort to make her mother feel better was one example of how Katie showed her mother empathy and understanding. When I asked why she thought Katie called her "Miss Dude" and Lolly "Mom," Carol said, "She knows it's a game. She'll say to me, 'Mom, I know that sometimes I call you Miss Dude, but I know you're my mom.'"

Carol's sense of Katie is that her daughter is intelligent, witty, sensitive, and worthy of friendship. During a conversation about Katie's unreciprocated efforts for peer friendships, Carol commented, "I think I feel sadder about it than she does. Really! You know, if it was me being in her shoes, I would be really sad." Carol imagined herself in Katie's circumstance, and she was able to understand how Katie might interpret her experiences.

## KATIE AND JIM: "SHE'S A REAL TEASER."

Katie's father affectionately calls her by different names. "I call her Judy and Jerry a lot," he said, and she calls him "Mr. Dude." "She's a real teaser," Jim told me. He believes teasing is one way Katie negotiates meaning and roles within relationships. Jim explained teasing as "a natural form of communication for [Katie]." He continued,

> I think, people who know her realize, I mean, I don't think she does that unless she is close to someone. I think, honestly, that's her way of testing out to see how close she is with somebody. [Assuming Katie's voice:] "Let's see if they really get me." Unfortunately, in her peer group a lot of kids that she socialized with I don't think have as sophisticated of a sarcasm palate as what she has, and they don't get the joke.

Jim makes two points in this remark. First, he suggests that Katie's teasing is her attempt to establish power within relationships. Second, his reference to Katie's "sophisticated sarcasm palate" implies recognition of Katie's intelligence. Thus, much like Carol, Jim views his daughter as clever (at least more so than those who misunderstand her).

Jim admitted, "It's hard to tell when she turns it into drama or when it's a real feeling. . . . Sometimes she's quoting a movie and it isn't real feeling, and it's just her dialect, her way of expressing it." Katie's brother, Randy, concurred, advising those who seek understanding to spend "one-on-one" time together over a long period of time. Jim thought that people sometimes misunderstood Katie because "they make it about them instead of about her." He added, "It exposes [their] insecurity."

To a certain extent, Jim placed the responsibility of negotiating shared meaning with Katie on the communication partner's level of "sophistication" and confidence. His sentiment was echoed by Randy, who said, "Katie is sort of a door that's open to everyone, and whether a reciprocal relationship can exist depends on whether a person she encounters is willing to walk through."

Jim also acknowledged that Katie "has a real problem with boundaries and keeping her hands off other people's stuff." Yet he also expressed a much deeper understanding of why Katie might have this "problem." He explained how the social service workers and school associates always touched Katie's stuff, so he thought it seemed reasonable that Katie had not learned social boundaries. He talked about Katie and other kids with disabilities served by these special systems: "These kids have a lot of handlers. . . . They're used to being invaded." Jim's ability to empathize with the social implications (and medical implications I referred to previously) of having trisomy 21 seemed to play an important part in his relationship with his daughter. He believes that "Katie's got a tough life ahead of her" and that his role is to prepare her for it. So again, like Carol, Jim has imagined life from Katie's perspective.

## KATIE AND LOLLY: "SHE'S IMPORTANT TO ME."

Forty-something Lolly was sipping her second coffee at the new bread and coffee house chain in Hutton when she shared her perspective of Katie with me. "She is smart. She is confident, especially for a teenager, but not cocky. . . . She's important to me." They had met a few years earlier at church. Katie and Lolly's son were in the same confirmation class when Lolly sponsored and then befriended Katie. "In the beginning, I didn't know her very well," Lolly explained, but since then the two families had become close, and they frequently shared Sunday evening dinners together. Lolly described a mutually beneficial relationship that developed over time between herself and Katie.

During a time when Lolly worked in Washington High's art department, Katie regularly joined her in her office before school started. Lolly described Katie as "endlessly joyful." She said that Katie's joy rubs off on her when they are together. Being with Katie "has forced me to be more easy-going," she explained. "She's just so free. . . . She's encouraged me to kind of let go of some things," implying that Katie has contributed to Lolly becoming a better person. Katie noted that sometimes she slept over at Lolly's and that they shared "special moments together" shopping and going to movies. She once said, "Me and Lolly are getting married." In the school context, this comment might have prompted a behavior intervention, but Lolly and those close to Katie understood this comment to represent only her deep affection for Lolly. "I would die without [Lolly]." Clearly, the two held each other in high regard.

Although Lolly benefited from her relationship with Katie, she also expressed concern about Katie's occasional "inappropriate" behaviors. "You know, sometimes you need to conform to fit into this society," she said. She referred to Katie calling her "Mom" and then asked rhetorically, "Can you imagine her life skills friends?" She thought that this must be confusing for them because they knew Katie's real mother. So on occasions when Katie called Lolly "Mom" in front of them, Lolly explained, "Then I always have to go 'Pretend Mom.'"

Lolly's impression that Katie's use of "pretend" names was a form of Katie's assertiveness was similar to Jim's interpretation that it was Katie's way of "teasing." "It's kind of like a form of teenage rebellion" toward her real mother, Lolly suggested. She likened Katie's name switching to a typical teen "slamming her door to her room." In other words, Lolly thought that when Katie called her "Mom" (especially in Carol's presence), she was actively participating in the process of seeking power. It follows then that both Jim and Lolly viewed Katie's use of language as conscious and as a tool for negotiating meaning and roles within relationships.

## KATIE AND ME: "MY HOUSE, MY RULES."

As her father suggested would be the case, at times I found Katie's communication difficult to interpret. He had said, "It's just hard to tell when she turns it into drama." For example, during one of our afternoons together, Katie and I went to get my car tires changed, and while we waited in the small sitting area, Katie suddenly stood up and began reenacting a scene. As was common with Katie, she held a small notebook, from which she read lines of a script she had written involving two characters. While I sat at one of two small tables and watched, Katie took the role of a person hiding behind an imaginary bush. The next moment she took the position of another person a few feet away, looking at the imaginary bush and telling the person behind it to come out. She easily switched back and forth between characters in the scene, changing both her posture and voice. In this situation, Katie appeared to be using her imagination simply to pass the time.

However, in another situation, Katie's song suggested deeper meaning, an attempt on her part to communicate her impression of me. It was one of my first visits to Katie's house. Her mom led me up the Victorian-carpeted wooden staircase, past the stained glass windows to just outside Katie's bedroom. We could easily hear Katie singing behind the closed door. "That's a song from *Wicked*," her mother explained, "the Broadway show we went to see in Chicago for her birthday." We entered her room while Katie continued to sing and dance, holding a broomstick that served both as a microphone and a dance partner. Later during the visit while Katie and I talked alone, she unexpectedly picked up her guitar and started to play and sing, "I know there is more inside you, Janet." Again, Katie's imagination revealed itself, but in this case she directed her attention to me and even incorporated my name into the song. Her choice of words in the context of two people just beginning to get to know each other made sense to me. Katie seemed to be both recognizing me as a fellow human being and telling me that she is someone who "knows" something "more" than what might first be obvious.

Katie's efforts toward building a reciprocal relationship with me began when we were sitting on a bench warming ourselves in the late spring sun. She stood up, threw her headband and the folder she had been carrying on the bench, and proceeded to skip over to a large modern fountain. She jumped back and forth over the fountain's runoff and challenged me to join her, risking a fall or getting wet. "Come on, Janet. You can do it." I followed her lead, though still somewhat apprehensive and aware of the passersby.

Several minutes later I tried to coax Katie into retreating back inside the building; instead she turned away and began whispering something to herself that I could not hear. I returned to the bench and waited, when finally she turned toward me and said, "Janet, I am going to come over and talk with you. Stay there." She then walked up to me with her hand outstretched and said, "Truce." I shook her hand and together we walked inside. This sign, early in our relationship, signaled to me her trust in me and our future as friends, a relationship that relied in part on shared risk taking and shared power.

Some of my initial efforts to try to negotiate meaning and power within my relationship with Katie became clear only after reviewing the transcriptions. For instance, one time we sat across from each other in a restaurant booth, Katie scooping vanilla ice cream and fudge into her mouth while I tried to engage her in conversation by asking her questions. All of a sudden she picked up the voice recorder from the table and said loudly, "Janet in her underwear. Yeah." The following conversation ensued:

J: [Let's talk about] something different.
K: Okay, now, what are you going to say about the underwear?
J: I'm sorry. I don't want to talk about that.
K: Why?
J: Because that's something that's just private. I don't talk with my girlfriends about that. And I don't do it at a restaurant. If I'm going to talk to my girlfriends about those things, I do it in private.
K: So you admit that I'm stupid?
J: No, I am saying that I'm asking you . . . [pause] like if I ask you something and you don't want to talk about it, we cannot talk about it.
K: And?
J: Are there things you . . .
K: [interrupting] But what makes you think that Mike . . .

Here Katie diverted the topic of conversation as she began to talk about Mike. In the conversation, I repeatedly tried to redirect the topic away from what I felt was uncomfortable in the context (a public setting). Katie asserted her power by taking the microphone and responding to each of my comments with her own questions. She seemed to challenge my attempts to regain control by asking if I thought she was stupid. At the end of this exchange, Katie interrupted me—another assertion—but this time she seemed to recognize my need to change the subject by introducing Mike as a new topic.

In her ensuing narrative, she said plainly, "Now, don't be sarcastic about this. I just want to say that I promise I won't ever say anything about this [i.e., the underwear] . . . because I want you to be more of as a friend to me, as well as anything." I interpreted these comments to mean that, first, she wanted to be taken seriously (by using the word "sarcastic" and changing her tone of voice) as a real friend; and second, that she was sorry if she had hurt my feelings and that she would try not to do it again. Katie again showed her interest in befriending me while we rode in my car and I told her "I'm not sure if I can do a good job telling your story." Katie accurately perceived that I was becoming emotional, and she asked, "Are you okay?" Her actions and words in these circumstances, much like when she broke out into song to cheer up her tearful mother,

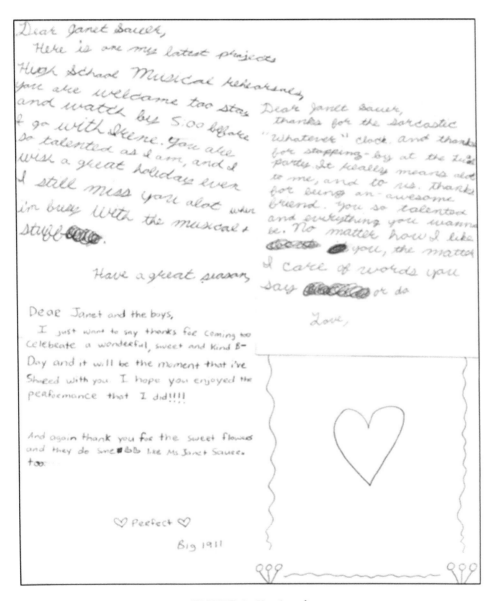

*FIGURE 6. Katie's cards.*

illustrate Katie's empathetic sense. Katie routinely wrote cards to me using a variety of printed and cursive styles that often featured her own heart drawings. She thanked me for visiting her or attending her theatrical performances and informed me about her latest "project." Her closings varied: "Have a great summer," "Love," or "Perfect." So although Katie's efforts to develop positive relationships are sometimes less than obvious, she asserts her interest in negotiating meaning and power and she displays empathy and understanding of others' feelings and needs.

One of Katie's more apparent negotiations with me included one of my visits to her house, when she insisted I join her in having dessert. "My house, my rules," she told me, handing me a large slice of banana bread covered in ice cream. She also was quick to remind me that we had a friendship with equal status on the occasion when her mother asked me to help Katie with some homework and I began to offer Katie suggestions for improving her paper. "You're not my teacher," she retorted, darting me an accusatory look. If she became disinterested in our conversation, she would sarcastically say, "and your point is?" Through her assertions, Katie has shown herself to be a person who deserves to be taken seriously (not "stupid"), a force to be reckoned with ("my rules"), and someone who is sensitive ("are you okay?"), imaginative, and worthy of friendship. She knows that in order to develop positive relationships, power must be negotiated and a "truce" is necessary.

## KATIE ON KATIE: "I HAVE A WONDERFUL LIFE."

During one of our initial coauthoring sessions, I suggested to Katie that she create a graphic web to outline her relationships with other people. Katie was familiar with using webs as graphic organizers for her school assignments. Atop the legal-sized yellow notepad I wrote "Katie's Story: Relationships with others." Then I drew a circle in the middle of the paper and wrote her name within it. At this point, Katie took control of the pencil, drew four lines out from the center circle, each in a different direction, and at the end of each line she drew a small circle. In the first circle, she wrote "Lolly"; in the second, she wrote "Randy"; in the third, she wrote the name of Lolly's dog; and in the fourth circle, she wrote "work." A few minutes later she added another line and circle, and in it she wrote "movies."

A week later when we met and I brought out this relationship web to ask Katie about it, she added a sixth circle. In this circle, she wrote the name of her classmate who was the lead in the spring musical earlier that year, the girl who played the part of Belle in *Beauty and the Beast*, the girl whose initial friendship with Katie had ended after Katie wrote her letters of affection that were apparently misinterpreted.

The three people Katie included in her web, Lolly, Randy, and Belle, are clearly some of the people she values. Note Lolly's relative status—the first name; even Lolly's dog is given a place of importance. Katie calls Lolly "Mom" and says they share "special moments," thus confirming the reciprocal nature of their relationship. Though I did not explore their sibling relationship in detail, Randy is significant to Katie. The addition of Belle could indicate Katie's refusal to accept the end of the relationship, an act of defiance similar to what Lolly called Katie's "teenage rebellion." It is worth noting that Katie might have continued to add (or remove) names to her friendship web if we would have revisited it.

Katie did not explain what "work" meant to the friendship web, but because she spent so much of her time writing and because her parents "worked" in the arts, it may have meant her art and theatrical "work." When Katie was given the opportunity for course electives, she chose art and photography, both classes in which she worked hard. The result of Katie's artistic and creative efforts can easily be seen in her self-portrait (see Figure 5) and the other paintings her mother framed and hung on the living room wall.

Kate was often in performance, whether singing, dancing, or acting out scenes based on her written reconstructions. Her closest friend, Lolly, first met Katie during a church service when Katie got Lolly to join her in dancing in the back, behind the pews. "I'm a good dancer," Katie announced, when she showed me her dancing talents in her living room, in her backyard, at the Christmas dance, and on the school stage. As I mentioned earlier, one time when Katie was dictating to me what to write about her, she told me, "Singing is what I do," and later she said similarly, "I am a pop diva!" Thus, Katie's reference to "work" and "movies" might be related in the same way that many people find their work to offer some pleasure. In other words, like the pop divas whom she adored, Katie worked on her movie or play scripts and then performed (or published) them.

Anyone who spends much time with Katie is likely to witness her ability to shift from conventional conversation into singing a song or playing a theatrical role. Her teacher thought this was an example of Katie's active imagination. I agree with her and with Katie's father, who suggested that Katie uses these pieces of dialogue or words from a song as a way to negotiate meaning and roles within relationships. Katie's use of script dialogue seems to provide her with a way to express her intended meaning when she finds searching for the "right" words difficult, or what Gee (1996) calls the "right lines" of a particular social discourse. She might just as well prefer the cadence, vocabulary, or style of play scripts.

I also concur with Lolly, who suggested that Katie's playfulness and sarcasm serve her need to assert herself. For example, during a bike ride we took together, Katie held the audio recorder and began singing, "It feels so great to be here with you. I'm Gabriella Montez." Looking over at me, she added, "and this is Troy Bolton and you are watching *High School Musical.*" Although Katie used the same names of the characters as those in the movie, she modified the script slightly, making it like an introduction to a show. Here she adopted the role of Gabriella, and she gave me the role of Troy, Gabriella's boyfriend, not bothering herself with gender. I think she was indeed happy to be spending time with me, and in this instance she used a piece of a familiar script, from a movie she had seen dozens of times and which she could probably recite verbatim, to express that happiness to me.

In addition to using the relationship web to learn about Katie's perspective on her life, I gave Katie the voice recorder to keep for a week. She recorded nearly 100 separate segments. She began one segment by talking about her family and how much she loved them and then said, "I have a wonderful life." Several of the segments included Katie reciting dialogue from scripts familiar to her. One segment I found powerful was when she recited the following words from *High School Musical:* "I never pretended to be somebody else. It's been me all along. . . . I can tell you that I know what it feels like to be afraid to show who you are." Perhaps here she was expressing her own frustration with vying for social acceptance.

Katie and I also conversed through e-mail, and one e-mail exchange revealed this struggle for acceptance. Katie wrote, "so far everybody treats me differently the way I am." When I asked her to clarify this in person, she repeated herself and then added, "Some of them know me and some of them don't." I interpret this to mean that she knows when people accept her for who she is, when they interact with her genuinely. Early in the study, Katie's mother said she thought Katie was not yearning for more friendships, but later she confided that Katie often returned home and immediately asked whether one of the girls from school had called. Katie's relationships with other students with whom she participates in Special Olympics, camps, or parties for students labeled with disabilities continue, but these are all organized and closely monitored by adults, and her relationships with typical students seem to be fragile at best.

During one series of recordings, Katie provided a lengthy description about her interests. This transcription reflects a typical teenager's interests, but its apparent simplistic use of narrative style might reinforce the negative stereotype often attached to people with trisomy 21:

Hi, I'm Katie. . . . So now I am here to tell you what my life really is. My favorite TV shows is *Hannah Montana* and *The Parent Trap*. My embarrassing moments is when I sing—I'll take a rain check on that. [Turns off the recorder]

Speaking of a rain check, I want to say that my favorite TV shows is *Hannah Montana* and *The Parent Trap*. My embarrassing moments is singing. When I act, I get stage fright. My dad videotapes my speeches. Austin is my [she alters her voice to make it high-pitched] boyfriend. [She reads from a list.] Now, my hobbies. Cleaning, organizing, horseback riding, writing, watching TV, and [name of coffee shop], which is where I am going today after this. Shopping, staying overnight at friends. Bowling, cooking.

Hanging out with friends at the mall. And cheerleading. My favorite color is orange and blue. My friends. [She names the social service worker who preceded Mary], Lolly. And my love at first sight, my lovely fiancé, Austin. My favorite movie is the star of my favorite movie, *Cinderella Story*.

Now the foods that I eat. Pancakes. Italian pizza.

Ice cream. Fruit. Purple grapes and salads. Now my favorite thing to drink. Orange juice. Iced tea. And smoothies. Grape juice and flavored water. Now, the names of people. Lolly is going to turn 46 this year. Me, being 18, then 19. My mommy is 46, but she's going to be that age . . . [yawn, cough, burp]. All you bad people, all do, do . . . [unclear].

And my dog, Bailey.

Katie's conversation about herself is not unlike something one might hear from any teenager. She talked about her favorite food, TV shows, and activities. She also mentioned that writing was one of her "hobbies." However, if this was the only means by which someone were to know Katie, they might conclude that she was not capable of more sophisticated writing or other forms of expression. In other words, as Katie's mother made clear in her interpretation of Katie's answers to the Foods II test, Katie is a far more complex thinker than people might initially recognize.

When she is given the opportunity to use her artistic and linguistic talents and when the content is meaningful, Katie shows her depth and rich understanding of the world and relationships with the people in it. Upon listening to Katie's recording, it was obvious that she was reading, likely from one of her many notebooks or scrapbooks, where she wrote pages upon pages about herself and people she thought about. She was often writing: letters, lists, cards, notes, or scripts. One day she and her mother filled nearly a dozen notebook pages writing back and forth in a style reminiscent of a "Dear Abby" column. While attending her brother's college symphony concert, Katie methodically circled certain words and crossed out others from the program. She also inserted a few words. Upon careful examination, it became evident she had created an entirely original coherent message from the existing text. She also purchased a Spanish–English dictionary and practiced translations in one of her notebooks.

In addition to the performing arts and more traditional forms of literacy, Katie has taken up photography and painting. Katie also is computer literate. She easily navigates the internet and other technology. She readily uses her own DVD player, and she quickly learned how to use my digital voice recorder, my video camera, and computer editing software. In school, Katie used her talents to create PowerPoint presentations, to prepare and present speeches, and to write and perform a rap song for her state report on Wyoming.

The people in Katie's life who know her well understand the powerful role literacy plays for her. For Katie's 18th birthday, Lolly gave Katie a collection of art supplies and an oversized handmade portfolio to hold Katie's completed works. Other guests gave her stationary, lined notebooks, and various writing instruments. Katie has always been encouraged to express herself verbally, visually, musically, theatrically, and through writing. These forms of communication appear to have contributed to Katie's sense of self, her confidence, and her ability to initiate (and sometimes maintain) meaningful relationships. Conversely, Katie's language use, such as incorporating play scripts into her discourse and apparent overzealous and affectionate letter writing, has not helped her efforts to develop some lasting peer relationships.

## EMERGING THEMES AND ASSERTIONS

*Language and Literacy as Precarious Social Tools*

People who know Katie well did not seem distracted by some of her unconventional speech patterns or dysfluencies. Rather, they seemed challenged by how to interpret her ways of communicating her thoughts and feelings or what Gee (1999) calls "language-in-use" (p. 45). When I first met Katie, I found myself asking her to repeat herself on a regular basis. At times, she read the confusion on my face and slowly repeated herself on her own. In some cases, Katie spelled the words that I could not discern in her speech. She was always patient with me, and she made considerable effort to ensure I understood what she was saying.

Over time, as I got to know Katie and became her friend, I found myself more challenged by some of her ways of communicating, which sometimes led me to be confused or embarrassed. Examples include her performance at the tire shop and when she kept saying "underwear" out loud at the restaurant. As her family and teachers expressed, Katie is quick to tease people she knows and likes, so I learned to either tease her back or to play along with her. She also interjects pieces of books and movie scripts into her conversations or monologues, which I found often served as carriers for deeper meanings. To discover her intended meaning I found listening more carefully (e.g., not rushing or allowing myself to be distracted) to be helpful.

Katie readily talks, sings, and writes about her affection for others. She also draws and paints beautiful pictures, which she then eagerly gives away. At times, these uses of literate forms seemed to serve Katie as means for developing more complex relationships. They allowed her a way to express herself and to give something to others, important aspects of reciprocal relationships.

Katie's interest in and facility with the written word seemed to elevate her social status in that it allowed her greater access to general education classes and participation in plays and choir, but other times it became a sort of liability. Her parents and close adult friends all described Katie as smart. Whereas I did not see typical students interact socially with other students labeled as disabled, Katie self-assuredly conversed with her nondisabled peers, making use of her relatively conventional speech. On several occasions, I observed Katie waving and greeting her typical peers in the halls, in classrooms during noninstructional time, during rehearsal, and outside after school. Each time the typical peers returned the greeting. Nonetheless, only once did I see a nondisabled peer initiate a greeting with Katie, suggesting that the level of acceptance Katie received may be inconsistent. "They're being polite, but they are not her friends," teachers told me. Because of the apparent fragile nature of Katie's relationship with the two girls outside special education, I did not interview them, nor was I able to observe them together, so I do not know how they negotiated shared meaning. However, Katie's greeting cards and verbal expressions of affection were the actions that jeopardized their relationships.

Unfortunately, Katie's literacy and language skills did not seem to carry as much social clout outside of her closer social circles. Despite the fact that Katie was having some academic success and she volunteered in the city library as part of her community service, when out in the community with her social service worker, Katie joined her peers as someone with "client" status. She and other clients were talked about in their presence. Although at least one purpose for their work was to encourage social skills in the community, to my knowledge, the only socializing Katie did with the social service worker was with other people with disabilities. "She's not very social," her worker said, suggesting it was difficult to support a more expansive social life for Katie. In this way, apparently because she was a receiver of social services, Katie's language and literacy skills were ignored.

Many people in Katie's life questioned her understanding of reality, and some people, including a few of her teachers, were particularly concerned about her use of fictitious characters and stories in her daily life. Although her high school English teacher recognized Katie's use of her imagination as something of value, she also qualified it. "She gets confused between reality and fantasy," the teacher asserted, before telling me the story about Katie adopting a classmate's name. As noted previously, frequently during my visits with Katie she abruptly changed from conversing with me or others to reciting scripts or words from a song. She also turned away, and as actors are trained to do, she appeared to imagine another person beside her with whom she then began a conversation. Her entire affect changed, including her tone of voice. She even paused, allowing time for her imaginary conversational partner to speak. Sometimes Katie performed both roles in a scene. Thus, although imagination is viewed as an important aspect to literacy (Gallas, 2003; Kress, 1997; Paley, 2004) and as a valuable creative tool, for Katie it was somewhat discouraged.

People who were regularly part of Katie's life typically made light of her teasing ways for referring to them. She often called her father "Mr. Dude," her mother "Miss Dude," and Lolly "Mom." She also called other adult female friends "Mom" on occasion. Katie introduced me to a few people at her school as her sister. On any occasion, she might refer to herself as one or more different characters from a play or movie such as she did on our bike ride when she said "I'm Gabriella." These comments, much like the answers Katie wrote on her Foods II test, seemed to more often confuse Katie's communication partners than allow for developing shared meaning or understanding. In summary, Katie's facility with language and literacy sometimes worked to her advantage in developing reciprocal relationships, and other times it worked toward their demise.

*Negotiating Power as Part of Developing a Reciprocal Relationship*

The contexts within which Katie was provided with opportunities to develop relationships were arguably limited by social and institutional interpretations of Katie that were based on her disability label. The "boxes" her mother referred to in special educational programming certainly restricted Katie's access to unlabeled peers, and in these classes Katie was given little power to make choices. Referred to vaguely as a person "on [an] IEP" and expected to wash windows or sweep the floor in a highly structured way, Katie's life skills program disempowered her. Similarly, the social service system socialized Katie as part of a stigmatized subgroup of people referred to as "clients," where talking about them in their presence was acceptable.

It seemed that some people interested in developing a reciprocal relationship with Katie (e.g., her family, Lolly, and me) became comfortable enough within the relationship not to be bothered by the socially "appropriate" expectations of conversations one might expect of an older teenager. Katie's family contends that the development of her reciprocal relationships "rests almost entirely on the other party," that the person needs sophistication and a "sarcastic palate" in order to negotiate shared understanding with Katie. I found a sound background and knowledge in theater arts and current pop culture to be helpful in interpreting Katie's communication.

Katie's family's explanation that so much of developing a reciprocal relationship with Katie rests with the other person and that other people she encounters either do not have a sophisticated sarcastic palate or knowledge about theatrical scripts might explain some of the reasons for Katie's successful and unsuccessful relationships. However, a relationship by definition is a partnership, and Katie also plays a role. As Lolly suggested, Katie was probably exerting some of her own agency, her own desires, and role preferences when she informed me that I was to follow "her rules" and that I was not her teacher. Her unconventional behaviors, such as acting out a scene in public, might very well have been part of her sharing her feelings at the moment with me, but they could just as likely have been her efforts to push me back a bit, to affirm her equal status in the relationship, to take the lead.

People who seem to share positive relationships with Katie interpret her in different ways, but with each relationship I examined, including my own, there seemed to include an element of risk taking on both sides. Katie asserted herself during conversations with me and others when she redirected the conversation to one of her own interests, when she took control of the voice recorder or the pen, when she stopped the conversation and corrected her communication partner, and when she completely dropped out of the conversation by turning away and taking on the role of a movie or play character. Relinquishing control of the conversation, the activity, or my research tools (i.e., my pen, notebook, voice recorder, computer) necessitated an acceptance of risk. At times, I feared Katie could break something or that I would not get the information I sought (without realizing at the time that by letting go I was in fact gaining more information about Katie).

Katie often asked in a sarcastic tone, "And your point is?" when she appeared no longer interested in someone else's topic of conversation. When she was sitting among her family and they began to dominate the conversation, she interjected, "Janet says I'm the leader in this story thing." On these occasions, I felt some anxiety that Katie might not feel comfortable enough with me to share her thoughts openly. I also considered the possibility that she might withdraw from the study and that led to some obvious concern on my part.

To summarize, Katie's confidence and willingness to take the emotional risk of engaging in complex social relationships was evident throughout this study. Successful, reciprocal relationships included risk taking and power sharing from both parties, Katie and her nondisabled friends and family. Her unconventional ways of using language and "being in the world" (Gee, 1999) sometimes jeopardized her relationships. Additionally, the restrictive nature of the social and educational service systems seemed to interfere with Katie's developing relationships. Katie's efforts to be taken seriously, viewed not as "stupid" but as someone who deserved attention and friendship, were met with different reactions. Those close to her seemed not to be bothered, and some even joined her in teasing, dancing in public, or other playful ways of being together and constructing shared meaning.

# CHAPTER 4

# Marie's Portrait

*FIGURE 7. Marie writes and draws a story.*

## MEETING MARIE: "EVERYONE LIKES BOOKS!"

One of my first visits to Marie's home made clear both the joy she got from engaging in the social aspects of book reading and her confident sense of self. Although I had known Marie before she became a participant in my study, I did not know her in any deep or personal way, and thus it was more like I knew of her. I had seen her in the halls of the small rural community school she attended and I had read an article about her in the local newspaper where she was referred to as the town's "silent angel," but until I joined her and her family in their recently built ranch-style home on the outskirts of Verstanburg, I had not experienced her squeals of laughter while sharing a book or the other ways she made her presence known.

At 8 years of age, Marie was the oldest of four: Scott, age 5; Austin, age 3; and Sara, the newborn baby. On this early summer visit, I found Marie's mother, Amy, "hanging out" with her four children and her 3-year-old nephew, Christopher. Amy was on maternity leave from work at the meat locker in town. The active children, detailed calendar, and lengthy to-do list indicated a busy household.

Amy called Marie to join us and the other children in Marie's newly painted pink bedroom. "I want you to come show Janet something." Marie was quick to respond. I did not discern the exact words until later when transcribing, but this was her first clear assertion: "I'm not coming." Despite her initial resistance, moments later, Marie joined us on the floor of her bedroom surrounded by books. "Everybody likes books," Amy said while the children sorted through piles of books, opening and closing them and selecting ones for me to read aloud.

Amy faded into the background as the children and I spent the next half hour or so cuddled up reading, giggling at the stories, and occasionally throwing our bare feet up into the air. I learned that when Marie was happy she often leaned back on the floor and playfully kicked her feet up into the air. The two older boys and Marie each picked out a book and pushed them into my lap. I read Marie's book aloud first, *Just My Friend and Me* by Mercer Meyer (2001), and then several of the other children's choices before coming to an oversized version of *Pat the Bunny*, the classic tactile book by Dorothy Kunhardt (1962). Marie handed it to me.

> J: [Beginning to read] "Paul and Judy . . ." What's that furry animal over there? [I point to the sheep picture.]
>
> M: Sheep. [She reaches over and hits the sheep picture.]
>
> J: Yeah. Do you want to get closer? Yeah, touch it. [The children lean in and touch the cotton ball piece glued into the book.]
>
> S: It's soft.
>
> J: Yeah, what does the lamb say? It's got the word here. BAaaa. And what's this? [I point to a kitten picture.]
>
> M: Kitty.
>
> J: That's right, Marie. It's not a bunny. It's a kitty. What sound does a kitty make?
>
> Kids: Meow.
>
> J: Yeah, pet her. She really likes that. Oh . . . my kitty likes it, right behind her ears and then she [making the purr sound]. There's another animal, what is it?
>
> M: [Turns the page and sees the dog.] Doggie.

    J: You said it, it's a doggie. [Reading again] "No, it's not a bunny. It's a fuzzy,
       furry doggie." Hello puppy. Little puppy. . . . [Each of the children takes
       a turn rubbing the fur. Then Marie reaches over and turns the page again.]
       Look, another furry animal. Now, is *that* a bunny? [pause] Is it?
  All: Yeah!

We returned to the book reading, but the children and I continuously interrupted the
reading of the texts to share personal related stories or to name things in the pictures.
Several times Marie asserted herself, by being the first to respond to my questions,
by interrupting me to comment on the story, and by putting her hand on the book
to slow me down or so she could more easily see the pictures and text. "I see," she
demanded.

    Marie exhibited familiarity with book reading routines in the above vignette. The
activity seemed to provide her with repeated opportunities for active joyful participation.
She showed confidence in her actions and words when engaged in reading in her home,
and as our shared time continued over the next several months, I saw this assurance
reemerge in many contexts.

## MARIE'S SOCIAL WORLDS: HER COMMUNITIES WRESTLE
## WITH DIFFERENCE

This section begins with a description of Marie's relationship with her neighborhood
community. Marie's membership in her community illustrated much of Kliewer and
Biklen's (2007) concept of *local understanding* and the positive construction of Marie's
humanness. Marie was not so much merely living in her community as she was of it. And
this relationship seemed to have positively influenced other contexts, such as school. At
the same time and in a somewhat contradictory vein, her community adopted the stereotypical expression "silent angel" to describe Marie, implying that she had nothing to
say and that she was incapable of doing anything troublesome. As such, the Verstanburg
community seemed to struggle with whether to interpret Marie's difference as a difference that mattered.

    The second context I describe is Marie's neighborhood school, where she spent most
of her time among same-age peers in the general education program. Here I include
additional educational contexts, such as summer school and Bible camp, where I observed
and interacted with Marie. The adults in these contexts acted in various situations as
Marie's advocate, protector, guide, interpreter, social monitor, and teacher. When people
viewed their role as protector, guide, and social monitor, they tended to be protective
and paternalistic. Other times, they listened carefully to Marie and interpreted her as an
individual with agency and a willful voice. They wrestled with these different roles and
related consequences. Marie negotiated her own role within these adult relationships; she

also negotiated peer relationships, which appeared to be influenced by the adults' roles and ways of interacting with Marie.

Marie's home life and family are described in the third part of this section. These descriptions of Marie's home life are limited to my own observations and interviews with her mother and grandmother; I was unable to interview Marie's father. Marie's family valued her membership and saw her as an independent thinker, a talker, and someone who enjoyed being "part of the action." They also struggled with their concern for Marie's safety and her paternal grandparents' apparent indifference toward her.

*Marie and Her Community: "The Silent Angel" of Verstanburg*

Both of Marie's parents worked away from home, but many families in the area still made their living off their own farms from a mixture of livestock, fields of grain, and large gardens. Verstanburg was known for its rodeo, which consumed this rural town for 3 days every summer. "Marie loves the rodeo," her mother told me after their family spent an evening there. Marie also enjoyed the town's swimming pool, playground, and library.

The town's 2000 census reported a population of 923, none of whom were foreign born, but nearly half claimed German heritage. The Chamber of Commerce quoted one business employer as saying, "Verstanburg's greatest asset is the small-town America atmosphere, where self-worth and pride in one's work is still held in high regard." If they were not working on their family farms, many high school students worked at the meat locker where Marie's mother worked. Hard work was clearly valued, but difference and disability seemed to complicate the idea of self-worth.

The Verstanburg newspaper regularly featured news about family gatherings, weddings, anniversaries, birthdays, obituaries, and school events. However, in their apparent effort to demystify Marie's difference, the newspaper featured two articles about Marie. According to the paper, Marie's mother, Amy, was concerned when she noticed that her daughter "was not talking as much as other 3 year olds." Years later, after having Marie's blood tested, Amy said the doctor called to tell them that Marie had the degenerative disease Rett Syndrome, which predominantly affects females and usually leads to increased physical and communicative difficulties and premature death.

One article title referred to Marie as a "Silent Angel," an expression the International Rett Syndrome Association has used to describe the girls' innocence and typical lack of spoken verbal skills. The article stated, "Amy believes that everyone who touched Marie's life is an angel. . . . All their friends, family, educators, and community have become Marie's Angels." In the article, Amy explained to the reporter that she wanted the community to help keep Marie safe and to "let Marie in." In a more recent article, Amy is quoted as saying, "I think it is important for Marie that the community that she lives in understands about a disease that controls her body." The family's openness regarding Marie's challenges and their call for the community to be part of Marie's support system reflected a trust among the people of Verstanburg that seemed to contribute to their way of interpreting Marie's identity. In this case, it meant accepting her as a member but also as someone who needed additional care.

The degree to which the newspaper articles influenced their readers' attitudes is unclear, but Marie's membership in her community was unmistakable. She regularly attended the local Catholic church services with her family, where she received the sacrament of First Communion. Marie also participated in weekly religious education classes. When she visited the local grocery store, the library, or the playground next door, adults and children alike exchanged greetings with her. She took music lessons from a neighbor and joined friends for birthday parties, Girl Scout outings, and summer Bible camp. Amy said of Marie that she "loves to be part of the action," a quality that was evident in school and community photos—where Marie was not set apart—that also appeared in the local paper.

*Marie's Schooling: Negotiating Social Roles*

The line between Marie's social circles in school and in the community was fairly permeable. Because many of the teachers and school staff were relatives of the school children, and it was a small elementary school, there was a strong family-like community within the school and during its related activities. The school boasted a nearly consistent 100 % participation in parent–teacher conferences. The elementary school served about 100 children in pre-kindergarten through sixth grade from Verstanburg, New Bergen, and the surrounding communities. There were only two class sections for Grades 2–6 and three sections for the early grades, where the teacher–student ratio was 1:15.

During my study, Marie transitioned from second into third grade. In the summer months, she spent two 2-week sessions in summer school and one 2-week session at Bible camp. Summer school was promoted and well attended, providing open enrollment for all interested students completing first through third grades. The curriculum was project-based, and small multiage groups rotated from one teacher and subject to another throughout the morning program. Marie's special education teacher, Miss Grant, taught in both summer school sessions and at Bible camp. A number of the special education associates who worked at the school during the year also worked at Bible camp; several of them were mothers and grandmothers of the school children.

The nondenominational Bible camp began each morning in the basement of the New Bergen Methodist Church, where the children were involved in crafts, Bible stories, cooking, games, and songs based on a daily Christian theme. The afternoons were spent traveling to various cultural activities in the area, such as a history museum and a nature center.

One hot July afternoon at Bible camp included a visit to a swimming pool in a nearby town. The pool was packed, and it took a minute for me to find Marie among the 70 campers and more than 100 other children. Wearing her pink-colored swimming suit, Marie splashed and laughed with her brother and other children in the shallow end. Later, I was sitting poolside with Miss Grant, who was putting a Band-Aid on a child's scraped knee when Mary, a slightly gray-haired associate, interrupted, holding Marie by the hand: "The lifeguard says she thinks Marie is too big to keep sliding with me. She thinks Marie could do it alone." The role of the associate and Marie's special education teacher (and thus Marie's competence as well) were being questioned by the larger community.

Without more than a moment's hesitation, Miss Grant decided they try it. She would meet Marie at the bottom of the water slide, and Mary would follow after her. So Mary walked up two stories of steps in the queue of wet, steamy children and stopped at the top. There she stayed, watching in anticipation as she took what she thought to be a risk, allowing Marie the opportunity to slide alone. Miss Grant turned to me, "We say we want her to be more independent—well, here goes." Together we watched Marie proudly descend the bright yellow slide, jump up out of the water at the bottom, and yell "I did it all by myself!" This incident illustrated how the adults' perceived roles influenced the opportunities Marie was provided to become increasingly independent. It also suggested an element of risk involved with letting go.

Miss Grant and the school support staff openly discussed their thoughts about Marie and her social interactions. They described risks they felt they needed to take, like letting her go down the pool slide alone, in order to provide Marie with opportunities to grow as an individual and member of the community. Miss Grant explained how "There were times we had real battles going down [to the special education room] because she kept wanting to be with the kids [in her regular class]." She continued in a self-deprecating way, "And it only took me like 3 to 4 weeks to figure out that she needed to be in the [regular] room . . . she's telling me this. Why didn't I pick up on it?" Miss Grant admonished herself for not listening deeply to Marie, who had used the nonverbal communication available to her at that time to express her preference to remain in the general classroom. Again Miss Grant had risked change in what had been the school's response to disability; rather than following the tradition of segregating Marie on the basis of her difference, Miss Grant listened deeply to Marie's call for social connection.

Miss Grant thought that her special education "training" had taught her to think of students like Marie as broken and that her role was "to fix them," suggesting that in situations like Marie's, this orientation meant "battles" rather than careful listening. Conversely, when Marie's special education teacher acknowledged Marie's will and listened to Marie's voice, Marie was then viewed primarily as a student or a third grader, and her disability lost its place as having master status (Becker, 1963; Taylor, 2000). The idea of letting go of traditional, clinical orientations toward Marie and recognizing Marie's right to active, increasingly independent involvement in daily social and academic life resurfaced repeatedly in Marie's life.

Miss Grant's new interpretation of Marie meant a constant challenge to the way she and other adults in the special education system interacted with Marie. Marie's will was not seen as worthy of recognition by all those who worked with her. The student teacher working with Marie under Miss Grant's supervision said, "It's hard building a relationship with her." She explained how she struggled with Marie's "behaviors" like when Marie lay on the classroom floor and asked her to read to her instead of working with the student teacher on the assigned task.

On several occasions, I observed Miss Grant assuring the student teacher and associates "Marie can do it" and "She'll be fine." Miss Grant appeared to advocate for Marie's increased independence by encouraging people to take the emotional, physical, and social risks involved with acknowledging Marie's capabilities and need for autonomy. In other words, Miss Grant's role changed once her orientation changed. She began to act as Marie's advocate, assuring others to accept the perceived risk of failure.

The school personnel seemed to wrestle with these different roles as Marie's advocate, guide, interpreter, social monitor, and teacher. The women hired as special education support staff often functioned as Marie's physical supports, guiding her ever-moving hands and unstable body through the daily routines of walking, writing, and opening and closing various things, including clothing fasteners, lockers, and pencil boxes. But by being nearly always present in Marie's school context, they constantly—and at times unknowingly—took on additional roles.

The associate Mrs. H. exemplified these conflicting roles and attitudes. When she viewed Marie as "the same" as typical students, she acted as Marie's advocate. She told another child concerned that Marie had nearly tipped herself out of her chair, "She's okay. She gets bumps and bruises just like the rest of you." Then she addressed me: "To me, all kids are the same. I treat all kids the same. . . . I don't care if they're special needs kids or not, that is just how it is." Conversely, Mrs. H. and several other associates who worked with Marie had developed strong, exceptional relationships with her that appeared somewhat paternalistic. A tender hug when passing Marie in the hall and a gentle pushing back of her hair from her face were examples of the special fondness school staff had for Marie. "I think the world of her," Mrs. H. told me.

This paternalistic affection toward Marie sometimes meant that the school personnel acted as Marie's "protector." The role of protector had real implications for Marie's educational opportunities. According to Miss Grant, during her weekly team planning meeting with Mrs. Perry, Marie's general education teacher, Mrs. Perry often said, "I think Marie can be in that class." At one such meeting, Miss Grant had questioned, "But why? I can't be in here that day." "It's okay," Mrs. Perry had reassured her, "*I'll* be there." In this case, Mrs. Perry acted as Marie's advocate, and Miss Grant was expected to relinquish some of her own responsibilities that fell under the role of protector. Thus, even though Miss Grant had changed her understanding of Marie, she continued to need reminders. "I have to watch myself. I have to back off," Miss Grant admitted.

Over time, Miss Grant and other school personnel began to change their understandings of Marie, and they became increasingly aware of how their attitudes influenced their roles, which then had real consequences for Marie's daily life at school. They made decisions to let Marie walk from the bus to her locker without an adult. Thereafter, Marie scampered among her classmates to the building, and spontaneous brief conversations emerged along the way. The staff agreed to leave Marie for longer periods of time on her own at her locker. The janitor modified the handle so she could open it by herself and she began taking off her coat and hanging it up independently. Inside the locker door, Miss Grant posted a series of Boardmaker pictures as a reminder of the steps Marie was expected to follow.

The adults' changes in attitude and role led to other consequences that influenced Marie's peer relationships. On the occasions when an adult was not with Marie at her locker, I observed Marie's classmates talking with her, sometimes offering to help her with her coat or backpack, other times just conversing about the day's activities. Thus, the awareness of the influence of their adult presence on Marie's interactions and independence led to changes that seemed to have a positive social outcome for her. In other words, when the adults relinquished some of their protector–supporter role and removed themselves from Marie's side, Marie experienced increased peer interactions and opportunities to be viewed as an equal communication partner.

Despite this level of awareness, however, there were times when I noted school staff speaking on Marie's behalf, instead of allowing Marie to answer for herself. It was as though their role as interpreters—for times when other people could not understand Marie—was transformed to speakers. For instance, when I asked Marie, "Are you done drying?" after she had washed her hands, without a pause the associate said, "Yeah, we're done." Not long afterward, I watched another associate sit beside Marie while talking most of the time and doing as much of the crayon drawing as Marie did on her paper. It was as though the adults assigned to support Marie sometimes took an increasingly important part in Marie's interactions, inadvertently forgoing her participation.

Similarly, when seeking Marie's involvement with certain more academic writing activities, school personnel provided her with choices of possible answers rather than have her generate her own work. This pattern of interaction seemed to have developed as a time-saving issue. However, as Miss Grant mentioned, Marie regularly asserted her own interests, using actions as well as words like "I do it self" and "Watch me, I do it." She often sought out opportunities to take control of writing instruments, especially since Miss Grant had given Marie a set of large, easy-to-grip crayons. One associate told me, "I sometimes have trouble with Marie's writing." In this case, not only did the associate wrestle with her role (Guide? Interpreter? Advocate?), Marie, too, struggled to be viewed as an active participant rather than someone who was helpless.

As part of their teaching role, the teachers and support staff regularly used their knowledge of Marie's interests and talents as well as their knowledge of Marie's family to create meaningful learning activities for Marie. When Miss Grant worked with Marie at a table in the special education resource room, sometimes she referred to the photographs of Marie and her family she had pinned on the bulletin board in front of them. Because Marie enjoyed singing, and swinging seemed to help her clarify her thinking, each morning after completing the initial homeroom activities, Mrs. H. and Marie walked down to an old locker room below the lunchroom, where Marie would swing and sing her spelling words and math facts. Miss Grant even found herself singing with Marie in the bathroom. This aspect of Miss Grant's and Mrs. H.'s teaching roles show how deep understanding and local knowledge of Marie was useful. It also served to validate Marie's individual identity.

In addition to the adults negotiating their roles as protector or advocate, speaker or interpreter, they wrestled with how much of their role as teacher involved being Marie's social monitor. They were working toward a balance between encouraging what they called Marie's "very social" and assertive personality and teaching her the "appropriate" formal school behaviors. "She'll be a great hall monitor," Miss Grant said. "She doesn't always talk a lot with the other kids, but she'll talk in the hallway. She'll say 'Walk kids!'" During a field trip where the children walked down steep stone steps, Miss Grant pulled Marie aside to let some other kids go by. As they passed, Marie told them, "Guys, careful. Watch step." In these instances, Marie used her facility with speech to assert herself as she negotiated her role among her peers but nearly always under the supervision of her adult social monitors.

My observations of Marie in school settings suggest that she successfully engaged in the formal educational discourse (Gee, 1999), oftentimes fulfilling the traditional student role. She followed the school routines of walking in the hall in a line from the playground into her class. She raised her hand and often correctly answered teacher questions. She cleaned up after herself in art and she used polite grammar, such as "Thank you." At times, she also yelled in the hall or balked at a teacher's insistence that she finish some school work, behaviors not altogether different from other, unlabeled, students.

Despite the school personnel's recognition of Marie's relative strength in socializing with others, in academic situations where an associate worked alongside Marie, I saw fewer interactions between her and her peers. Although Marie was part of a group in these situations, she tended to follow or stand at the back with an adult. When Marie was without an associate, however, as when she played at the community playground, I noticed a marked increase in Marie's verbalizations: "C'mon, play!" "I here. Where are you?" "Hey, watch this. I do that, too." She sought out peers to play with by calling their names and asking them (and me) to look at her or to come and play. Also, in academic contexts when Marie was without an adult, her peers more readily approached her, touched her, and talked to her. But these peer interactions were also influenced by the children's observations of the adult's roles and subsequent interactions with Marie.

In other words, Marie's classmates also seemed to wrestle with what they perceived were their roles and relationships with her.

Consequently, Marie's peer interactions included a mixture of what appeared to be typical conversation and play with what seemed to be less than equal relationships where she was viewed as someone in need of help. In the latter case, Miss Grant expressed her concern about Marie's peers; "Some kids also need to back off," she said, referring to classmates who regularly told Marie what to do and not to do or who tried to hold her hand in situations Miss Grant thought were unnecessary.

Miss Grant also noticed how Marie's classmates were developing their social awareness alongside her. "Watching the kids as they matured with [Marie], well, it's pretty awesome to see how they respond." She continued:

> They know that she can't do as much as they can, but they also know that she can do a lot of good things. In fact, at lunch last winter I was sitting with [a boy] who said, "Marie can add doubles and zero. She can color and write her name." He wasn't listing anything she couldn't do. He was listing everything she could do.

As Miss Grant noted, many of the children who were familiar with Marie had developed a deep understanding of Marie where she was accepted as a member of their class. They seemed to take no notice of her near-constant motion, and they intuitively involved her in activities, particularly when she was unaccompanied by an adult.

Within the school context, then, Marie actively negotiated her role as student and peer. She sought equal status within the general education environment through use of actions and words. The school personnel seemed to be working out their own relationships with Marie as they negotiated their ever-changing roles as teacher, guide, interpreter, advocate, and social monitor. Her classmates, too, wrestled with their roles, often taking cues from the adults around them.

*Marie's Family: "My side of the family accepts her for who she is."*

For the most part, Marie was viewed by her family as an individual and active member. She played with her siblings and relatives at home and in the neighborhood community. They knew her to be far from a "silent" little girl, and they respected her assertions. Yet like the school staff and larger community, they sometimes struggled with unaccepting attitudes within the extended family toward Marie's differences.

Marie's father, Kenny, grew up on a farm not far outside Verstanburg, but at the time of the study, he worked in one of the bigger towns about 15 miles away. Amy doubted I would get a chance to talk with him because he worked "quite a bit" building modular homes. Indeed, when I visited their home, he was usually at work, hunting, welding in his garage, or maintaining a large vegetable garden in their backyard.

Marie's paternal grandparents still lived on the family farm, and they were a regular feature in Marie's life, although Amy and Kenny noticed that his parents did not interact with Marie in the same way that they interacted with their many other grandchildren. With watery eyes, Amy retold a story to me about a recent visit to her in-laws where they seemed to have avoided Marie for the entire day. "Before we left, Marie went up to her grandma on her own and gave her a hug." Referring to her mother-in-law, she added, "If she only knew ..." before her voice trailed off. Amy was apparently perplexed by what she saw as her in-laws' insensitivity toward Marie's need to be acknowledged and loved. According to Amy, Kenny thought his mother would "come 'round" with time. The grandparents' attitude toward Marie was the one exception I found to an otherwise accepting family community.

Amy's parents had recently retired and bought a home in Verstanburg, where they had become a significant part of Marie's life, often meeting her at the school bus and taking her to weekly therapy sessions nearly an hour's drive from home. On their long drives, they often listened to music while Marie had a snack. "But yesterday," her grandma relayed, "Marie said 'No, talk' [meaning she preferred not to listen to music]. So we talked all the way there." Marie's grandma recalled another trip to the city for therapy when they stopped briefly at a ski hill. "She got so excited. 'I do it!' That's all she said over and over again." Marie's grandparents clearly viewed her as a vocal person interested in the world around them.

Amy discussed her family's relationship with Marie. "I don't think I could have had four kids and have a full-time job, by myself," Amy said, explaining how her return to work meant a greater reliance on her parents for child care. "My side of the family accepts her for who she is," Amy told me. She continued, "All of my brothers' kids treat her as one of them. If she's there, she's there. If not, she's not." Amy indicated here that her mother's sentiments were similarly shared by other extended family members.

As the opening vignette to this chapter illustrated, all of the children played together. They enjoyed hide-and-seek, reading, drawing, and especially swinging, whether on the backyard swing set or on one of the two swings that hung from the first-floor joists in the basement. Some Saturdays Amy took the kids "garage-saling," something she said Marie liked to do. "She was a chatterbox," Amy said, referring to Marie's speech while at the garage sales. "She was looking through a bunch of movies and picking one out for grandma, one for her little brother, and one for herself," Amy told me with a laugh. Her comments suggested that in contexts meaningful to Marie, her daughter talked a great deal.

Although Amy sought Marie's acceptance beyond the immediate family, she also struggled with how to address some of Marie's special needs. Amy became increasingly involved with Marie's educational program and related supplemental services. She held some of her own garage sales, along with other fundraisers, for Rett syndrome research. She attended research conferences with Kenny and Miss Grant about Rett syndrome and autism. She closely monitored Marie's schooling. Miss Grant referred to Amy as "a great mom," but Amy responded, "I'm just a mom. I'd do the same things for my other children." Amy acknowledged that for Marie, "Sensory is a big thing. Sensory input exhausts her by the end of the day," so Amy had added supplemental therapies for Marie. The therapists "suggested we roll her in a blanket, tightly, and brush her hard every two hours, deep pressure to help with her balance throughout the day. . . . It's hard to keep it integrated with school." She also was concerned about the inconsistent supervision of Marie on the bus for safety reasons. Amy's comments illustrate the complexities involved when addressing Marie's uncommon needs while at the same time accepting them as "just" part of the everyday life of parenting.

However challenging some aspects of addressing Marie's special needs might have been for her parents and maternal grandparents, they still did not seem to waiver in their acceptance of her. "[Marie] loves to have her hair done" and "her looks are important to her," Marie's grandma explained:

> She likes to look in the mirror. She'll flip back her head. She's got a new haircut now and I've been curling it each morning. . . . On the weekends she gets into it at home with Amy. She gets into that Body and Bath glittery stuff. She's kind of a shoe freak. She likes clothes. I guess every little girl will.

As her grandmother's description of Marie illustrates, in some of the most fundamental ways most of her family viewed Marie as just like any other little girl or family member. Like many of her siblings, "Scott watches out for [Marie] on occasion," Marie's grandma explained, "But I also see it the other way, too. They talk back and forth."

Thus, Marie's membership within her family was not in question, and their relationships were reciprocal. Her family openly described the influence of Rett syndrome on Marie, and they recognized the challenges of providing and coordinating her supports. But they seemed most concerned with her full acceptance as an active member of the extended family and the community at large.

## WAYS OF KNOWING MARIE

Although Marie was referred to in the local Verstanburg newspaper as "the silent angel," those close to Marie knew her as an assertive, vocal little girl. It was unclear why they adopted this adjective to describe her, but the contrast between the expression and Marie's actual characteristics symbolizes the tension between accepting Marie as a full human being worthy of being listened to and recognized as a family and community member and the stereotypical view of her that emphasized her difference, set her apart, and placed her in a position of lesser status.

*FIGURE 8. Brenda's drawing of Marie and her playing in a leaf pile at the park.
Janet, the researcher, is pictured standing waving to the girls.*

*Marie, Her Mother, and Her Grandmother: "You're not trying to work with a syndrome; you're trying to work with a little girl."*

When I first discussed Marie's communication with her mother, Amy declared, "She uses verbal communication. That's her main way of communicating." I had not noticed Marie's speech, and I saw her struggle with feeding herself at school, so I was initially doubtful about Marie's use of speech to communicate. Later Amy explained, "She uses minimal language to get her point across. . . . I wish others sometimes did that." So immediately upon introducing me to her daughter, Amy sought to dispel any notion of Marie being silent. Amy acknowledged Marie's intermittent use of speech, but she did not view it as important; rather, she viewed it as a positive characteristic.

During shopping visits to the town's single grocery store, Amy said, "If they ask her a question and she doesn't answer, they don't mind. She might answer, but she might not. They all act as if she understands anyway. We're known in the community and that helps." Amy's emphasis on being "known" in the community and how local people "act as if she understands" illustrates characteristics of local understanding (Kliewer & Biklen, 2007). She seemed to suggest that familiarity challenges the stereotype.

In addition to valuing Marie's way of communicating, her mother and grandmother also made use of a deeper, contextual knowledge of Marie in order to interpret her meaning. When the Make-A-Wish Foundation was scheduled to visit and interview Marie, Amy confided, "Others can't just listen to her to understand," reiterating the importance of familiarity when interpreting Marie. When I asked about using the picture communication that the school sometimes used to help with negotiating shared meaning, Amy dismissed it because of its limitations. As an example, she explained how when they tried to use pictures to help Marie learn prayers for church, Amy looked long and hard for an image in the Boardmaker program that would represent "God." "I'm glad that's over," she said, exasperated. "I mean, what do you use for 'God'?"

Marie's mother and grandmother found ways of interpreting Marie's sometimes unconventional communication by seeing her individuality within contexts. "In order to figure her out you need to get to know her, not the syndrome," Amy advised. "You're not trying to work with a syndrome; you're trying to work with a little girl." Marie's mother and grandmother knew that Marie was a better communicator in the morning and with routine and that she used her eyes for subtleness and "her hands stop clapping when she's focused." They consistently talked directly to Marie and waited for what might feel like an awkwardly long time for Marie to respond.

One day after I returned Marie to her grandparents' house, Grandma "Aga," as Marie called her, asked Marie whether she had fun. "No!" she answered firmly. Having spent the last few hours with Marie and her friend Brenda at the park, where I watched them laugh and play, I was perplexed. Then Grandma Aga explained to me that "That means she didn't want it to end." She told me not to take it personally, because Marie always got quiet or "growley" when she was unhappy with finishing something she enjoyed. However, another incident illustrates how Marie's words took on different meanings depending on the circumstances. When helping Marie decide what to wear, Grandma Aga explained, "You can tell. She won't put it on. She'll say 'No' to some things her mom picks out." In this case "No" meant No. The explanations offered by Grandma Aga and Amy illustrate the complexity of Marie's communication and the importance of familiarity. Also, they show Marie's use of language to affirm her role as an opinionated person.

Even when Marie did not speak, she was typically brought into conversations by her family, and her nonverbal communication was interpreted as meaningful. In one newspaper article, Marie was pictured laughing, her eyes facing the camera, her round, tanned face and dimpled cheeks outlined by thick eyebrows and shoulder-length light brown hair. Within the article, Amy described Marie this way: "Her big brown eyes will melt your heart and she definitely communicates a lot with her eyes."

Grandma Aga described her relationship with Marie as "real special." "I get very good hugs and that eye look I know. She can read my mind." These comments suggest a deep shared understanding between the two of them in which Marie's grandmother recognized her granddaughter's individuality and her contributions to their relationship. In this way and in the following excerpts, their relationship exemplified Bogdan and Taylor's (1987/1989) sociology of acceptance, in which the nondisabled person (a) attributes thinking to the other, (b) sees individuality in the other, (c) views the other as reciprocating, and (d) defines a social place for the other. Grandma Aga continued:

I spend a lot of time with her and I have a better understanding of her routine. She can also have her ornery times, but she wants approval from me, like other kids. . . .

It's a feeling you have with a grandchild, a bond, you learn to read every child. Marie wasn't always real vocal . . . she wasn't for a long while. She'd do a lot of screaming, ear-deafening. Like once at McDonald's . . . there was a woman who got offended by Marie's squealing with happiness. It was hard for me, but that was Marie's way to express herself. [The lady] didn't say it to me directly . . . people don't understand. That's just the way it is.

Marie's grandmother seemed to acknowledge Marie's right as a full member of the family and the wider community to express her "happiness" by whatever means she had available. In a separate incident where Grandma Aga thought she had lost Marie while at a department store, she explained how Marie "felt so bad" about upsetting her grandmother, illustrating Marie's empathy.

Another aspect to Grandma Aga's and Amy's relationships with Marie that is not captured by the theory of the sociology of acceptance (Bogdan & Taylor, 1987/1989) is the element of risk. Grandma Aga conceded to feeling emotional risk in her comment "It was hard for me" when she was at McDonald's. "People don't understand" reflects her struggle with the larger societal view that seemed not to understand Marie as a valued member. Both she and Amy felt at times that they had put Marie at physical risk of injury or of getting lost.

Despite knowing that the clinical prognosis for Marie's future was dim, both Grandma Aga and Amy expressed their optimism for Marie's continued development. Grandma Aga said, "She's got the world at her feet." Marie's mother and grandma saw the value of Marie's contributions to their relationships and her relationships with others. Amy wished other people might be more like Marie—by using fewer words to get their ideas across—instead of seeing her as deviant or less than human. Their relationships of local understanding seemed to act as models for others in the wider community to emulate.

*Marie's School Teachers: Miss Grant and Mrs. Perry's Chemistry*

Marie's third-grade teachers who co-taught Marie's class in math on a daily basis seemed to each have developed positive reciprocal relationships with Marie. Miss Grant, the 30-year veteran special education teacher, described Mrs. Perry's relationship with Marie as having "chemistry."

Miss Grant pointed out that only in recent years had she begun to work with children like Marie with more complex needs. She was intrigued by Rett syndrome and readily sought out information to learn more about it and ways that might help her work with Marie. She was on a Listserv for parents of children with Rett syndrome, and she referred me to books and articles she had received from Marie's mother. Miss Grant acknowledged, "I'm not sure there is a 'typical' Rett's girl," the first indication that she was willing to challenge some of the popular stereotypes.

Miss Grant spent a lot of time thinking about ways to improve Marie's quality of life. "Anything she can do to music sticks," she told me. One day they made up a song. She sang it for me: "Imagination means pretend. . . . You can be anything you want to be." She used a lot of books to teach Marie because she knew how much Marie enjoyed them and because they "quieted" her hands. She also initiated co-teaching at the school, where she regularly adapted the regular education curriculum with Mrs. Perry. In these ways, Miss Grant showed that her view of Marie was one that saw intelligence and talents and an ability to learn.

Miss Grant was very introspective and willing to change and challenge herself. She expressed a feeling that co-teaching and constant attention to modifying the curriculum required her to take some risks. One risk involved trying novel ways to help support Marie's learning. "When she was in first grade," Miss Grant recalled, "we would do a walk after lunch" as a way to "get her out of the building, to get her to talk." "We worked on greeting people and opening doors [and] we'd see a vehicle go down Main Street and I'd say, 'Where do you think that truck is going?'" They walked and talked through the small town of New Bergen. Occasionally Miss Grant let Marie walk her dog because Marie seemed to talk a lot to it. Marie's family dog had died, and Miss Grant thought that her dog "filled that gap. [The dog] is very soothing for Marie."

Similar to Marie's mother and grandmother, Miss Grant described Marie's speech as sometimes difficult for others to interpret because context and familiarity played a big part. For 3 years, Marie could not articulate Miss Grant's name, something Miss Grant had "gotten used to" and found endearing. "She says 'No' to a lot. Are you having a good time? [She imitates Marie.] 'No.' She *is* having a good time, but she just says 'No' a lot." Marie's teachers thought that she "gets stuck" trying to speak now and then, so Miss Grant used the book *Brown Bear, Brown Bear* (Martin & Carle, 1967) as a formulaic way "to get her talk" by prompting her with "What do you see?" Although she admitted "it's very rote," she defended the practice as "a way [Marie] does language." These comments illustrate how Miss Grant recognized Marie's particular language use without admonishing it, and at the same time she used Marie's interests to continue working on Marie's language and literacy development.

Miss Grant described Marie as "very alert" and "compassionate," asking after absent students and teachers. She said Marie was also "strong-willed" and someone who "wants to be independent." She thought that Marie's "buckiness" was related to her need for some control in her life. In this way, she said, "[Marie] is a very typical kid." Both Miss Grant's recognition of Marie's interest in becoming increasingly independent and her respect for Marie's natural need for autonomy highlighted important aspects to positive relationships. Such a perspective allowed Miss Grant to develop expectations of Marie that were similar to those for other children. In the weeks before school began, Miss Grant told me, "[Marie's] going to be a third grader, so she needs to grow up and have more grown-up kinds of expectations."

Seeing Marie's individuality, intelligence, and meaningful agency meant questioning stereotypes and traditional ways of interpreting and working with children with disabilities. Miss Grant explained, "The frustrating thing for me and for a lot of people is that *she knows*." She continued, "I firmly believe that she is understanding more than we are getting out of her, but that it's sort of trapped. She's not able to get it out, what she understands." This acknowledgment of Marie's intelligence led Miss Grant to question "the old IQ tests" and admit "I just don't know her learning possibility." Another day Miss Grant offered three instances of different teachers discovering things Marie knew. She then asked rhetorically, "How many things can Marie do that we don't know that she can do?"

Because she could not reliably assess Marie's knowledge and skills, Miss Grant found much of the IEP paperwork frustrating and less than relevant. "It's like a hoop you jump through." She questioned the practice of goal writing based on a child's disability. "How much are you looking at her *ability*?" A consequence of disability labels, she thought, seemed to put the students' possibilities for developing positive relationships with children and adults at risk. "You don't need a label. You can teach them without a label," she argued. Thus, Miss Grant found fault with the special education system and its practices on the basis of her local knowledge of Marie. This suggests an important aspect to local understanding: that it provided Marie with far more possibility than other ways of understanding her might otherwise have presented.

Mrs. Perry, another veteran teacher, was Marie's general education teacher for third grade. She did not respond to my requests for an interview, so the description of her relationship with Marie was limited to my observations and other people's comments. According to Marie's mother, "Marie attached right away to her teacher this year." Marie arrived home from school and reported to her mother everything her teacher did that day: "Perry did this, Perry did that." Miss Grant said, "There's something there with Mrs. Perry, a chemistry that's really been very special for Marie." On one of their field trips, I noticed Marie calling for and moving over to be with Mrs. Perry. "Perry, look!" she yelled, seeking her teacher's attention and calling her to join her as she pet a rabbit. During another school trip, Mrs. Perry was standing among several students in a small room when Marie entered, maneuvered herself through the children, and stopped just in front of Mrs. Perry, declaring "I here!" Later that day Marie joined a group of her classmates playing in a historical schoolhouse. Marie moved to the front, stood in front of the teacher's desk, and announced "I teacher." Marie's actions and words affirmed her interest in developing a relationship with Mrs. Perry.

Like Miss Grant, Mrs. Perry held high expectations for Marie. Amy explained, "Mrs. Perry will just say to Marie, 'You can do it,' instead of waiting for an associate." Mrs. Perry increasingly took a leadership role in Marie's education, inviting Miss Grant to join her in the general education classroom but also teaching Marie directly and advocating for Marie's independence as well. She frequently acknowledged Marie's efforts by awarding her one of the weekly all-school student awards. However, I did not notice Mrs. Perry pay any special attention to Marie, nor did I observe her ignoring Marie. Mrs. Perry seemed to accept Marie as a rightful member of her class in spite of her special learning needs.

The positive and respectful attitude Mrs. Perry and Miss Grant shared for Marie may have influenced others' ways of conversing with and around Marie in school. I observed many people talking to and about Marie in ways that did not patronize her, nor did they always assume their interpretations were correct. Associates made comments such as "It looks like she likes it," when Marie held a stuffed frog up to her face, or "I guess not," when instead of verbally responding to a question Marie handed the associate back a toy. Thus, Marie seemed to have developed positive reciprocal relationships with her teachers that managed to set a tone of acceptance and respect within the school environment.

*Marie and Neighbors Brenda and Patty: "The thing Marie likes to do most is sing!"*

In addition to experiencing positive relationships at home and at school, Marie was involved in positive reciprocal relationships in her neighborhood community as well. Here I describe two of them: Brenda, a demure blonde-haired third grader who lived a few blocks from Marie, and Patty, another neighbor who knew Marie through church and music lessons.

Brenda referred to Marie as her "friend." She invited Marie to her birthday party and was surprised to learn it was the first such party Marie had attended. She also brought Marie as her guest to a prayer group meeting. She seemed to make a point to approach Marie during class field trips and school events like the spring festival, where they greeted one another and just hung around together. Brenda readily joined Marie on the playground at school and in the neighborhood. At Grandma Aga's announcement that Brenda was going to join Marie at the park, Marie jumped up from the couch, smiled enough to show her dimples, and yelled "Brenda!" Clearly, the two girls shared a positive relationship.

I joined Brenda and Marie at the park and library, where they appeared to negotiate shared meaning without difficulty. They took turns in conversation and with choosing what activity to do. In the library, the two girls played with puppets made from children's books. Then Brenda asked Marie, "What do you want to do?" Marie answered clear as day: "I don't know, read!" So the two girls shared books and magazines. When Brenda joined some other kids in playing tag, Marie called, "Brenda! I do that, too." Later Marie said to Brenda, "I here. Look at me. . . . I watch you. You do it, hey, you do it." Here, Marie used oral language to assert herself and maintain an ongoing interaction with her friend.

Although Brenda had known me for 3 years prior to the study, she was hesitant to talk with me about her relationship with Marie, but she was quick to agree to draw me a picture of them together (see Figure 8). The detailed drawing shows the girls playing in a leaf pile at the park with me waving to them. There is nothing in the picture that portrayed Marie as anything other than just another girl, her friend.

The energetic mother of six and a children's book author, Patty Walsh taught piano, guitar, and a few other instruments to the children of Verstanburg and New Bergen. Patty and her music student Marie had developed a strong positive relationship that led Patty to write the articles about Marie for the local newspaper. Considered "a local," Patty was an active member of the community. For years she directed, designed costumes, and built sets for the high school plays. She was involved with the Parent Teacher Association, Girl Scouts, and the library. Although Patty had strong local sensibilities, she regularly traveled to cities across the country and abroad. She and her husband had also hosted a Japanese student a few years previous. So in some ways Patty was not a typical local Verstanburger, and these less usual qualities might have influenced her perspective of Marie as a valued community member.

Occasionally during the summer and every Friday after school in the fall, Marie went to Patty's house for music lessons. One fall Friday afternoon I joined them for one of their sessions at Patty's house. Throughout the next hour or so, I noticed the way Patty and Marie conversed and how Patty directly addressed Marie, asked her questions, and responded to Marie's comments and movements. If Marie did not immediately respond to Patty's questions or she answered "I don't know," Patty waited, rephrased her question, or carefully observed Marie's body and face in an effort to interpret Marie's intent. Patty never raised her voice or showed any tension in her body or voice to suggest frustration. Neither did Patty teach music from a prepared lesson plan, so she easily adjusted, moving from playing the guitar in the rocking chair to playing on the baby grand piano alongside Marie. "We've tried different instruments," Patty said, "but the thing Marie likes to do most is sing!"

That day they sang prayers Marie had learned for church and a number of interactive songs like "Bingo," in which Marie and Patty took turns leading the song. Marie also asked questions—"What is that?" referring to pictures in the song book and "Who is that?" in reference to the family dog barking or children's voices from other places in the house—and joined Patty in singing and taking her turn playing the instruments. Their communication took on a rhythm of its own whereby each of them took part, thus shar- ing the power and direction of their interaction. Both of them appeared comfortable in the other's presence, and they seemed to genuinely enjoy their time together.

Patty explained that Marie "likes to sing for people" and that she learned through music. According to Patty, the previous year Marie had learned many difficult prayers once they were put to music. Patty took the prayers Marie was expected to recite by memory and worked with her to learn them by singing them. Marie learned them quickly, faster than others in her class, so Marie and Patty then used the music to teach Marie's peers. "It was very exciting because she knew it before they did," Patty told me. She turned to Marie and asked, "Do you remember?" Then Patty began singing the prayer and gesturing with her hands. At first Marie hesitated, but then she joined Patty, the two of them singing, gesturing, and occasionally laughing together in front of me.

The manner in which Brenda and Patty interacted with Marie struck me as being so relaxed. I did not see the tension or struggle evident in the other relationships I described. They laughed, played, read, and sang together in such a way that Marie's differences did not seem important. My observations of their communication showed the importance of waiting, expecting a response from Marie, and responding to her so that meaning and power were shared. Finally, both Brenda and Patty seemed to have endeared themselves to Marie, which highlighted the significance of reciprocity.

*Marie Demands to Be Acknowledged: "Look at me!"*

Marie was empowered by her use of verbal language and various forms of literacy. She continually and in several contexts used verbal and written language to express herself and negotiate relationships. Occasionally, depending on how other people interpreted her assertiveness, Marie's use of language and literacy got her into trouble.

Although Marie had been called a "silent angel," her mother said she could be a "chatterbox." Despite Marie's difficulties with articulation, her brevity of speech, and her occasional silence, Marie was conversant with many forms of social dialogue. She said "Excuse me," "Thank you," and "Your turn" in situations considered "socially appropriate" (Gee, 1999). Repeatedly, in many circumstances, and with a number of different conversation partners, Marie seemed to successfully engage in verbal discourse. She listened and responded to other people's verbalizations, especially when it involved books, writing, or music. She learned math, spelling, and prayers through song. In a recording her mother made of Marie's running commentary while completing her homework one evening, Marie seemed to repeat the words she wrote and the directions the teachers gave her: "Okay, now . . . next." Thus, Marie seemed to make use of language to make meaning out of the world.

Marie also asserted herself by using her verbal skills. On the last day of summer school, the children were gathered in front of the large fish tanks near the front office, where the teachers handed out certificates of attendance and goodie bags. As the teacher called children's names, Marie shot up her hand, calling, "Me? Me?" Previously I mentioned how oftentimes Marie sought engagement by yelling "Look at me." During a brief one-on-one session with an associate in the special education classroom, Marie insisted that the associate take a turn ("Your turn"), and when it was Marie's turn, with the same intensity, she said, "I do it self."

As part of her language expressiveness, Marie liked to create stories using writing, books, and song. According to one of Marie's associates, "she can write her name, if you just lightly rest your hand over hers." Marie's mother explained the nuances of her daughter's writing: "That's how she makes her [letter in her name]." At the library one summer afternoon, Marie told me about her boat ride on the "Sippi" River while drawing what looked like blue wavy water lines on some paper (see Figure 7). Later, her mother corroborated Marie's story, and she clarified some of my questions about what Marie said and drew. Close examination of Marie's writing shows her knowledge of letter formation and direction. As was customary for Marie when provided with paper and writing instruments, at the library she covered the paper on both sides.

As the opening scene illustrated and many other people I interviewed reiterated, Marie loves books. She was familiar with the social routines involved with books, such as scanning and selecting a book from a shelf at the community library or orienting the book in her lap or on a table in front of herself or between herself and another person. She pointed to words in books and in the environment, saying them aloud, and she asked questions about words and pictures in books, such as "What's this?" As Patty said, Marie also loved to sing and did so enthusiastically during school concerts, religious education classes, Bible camp, and on car rides with her grandparents.

Marie's active participation and interest in books, writing, and music seemed to contribute to her social acceptance as a member of the literate community. What is interesting, however, is that Marie's language skills and literacy interests also sometimes got her into trouble. On field trips, her spontaneous vocalizations led adults to repeatedly tell her to "Shhh." The student teacher said that one day Marie had "laid down on the floor in class and said 'Read to me.'" Instead of following the student teacher's instruction, Marie's comment and action led to a confrontation between them. On another occasion, an associate had said, "I'm having trouble with her always wanting to write."

Whether Marie's actions or words got her into trouble seemed to depend on the context and the way people interpreted her. When Miss Grant finally realized that Marie's "battles" could be interpreted as meaningful communication and she recognized Marie's need for control and autonomy, she began to build a more positive relationship with Marie with deeper understanding. Similarly, when Marie hid from her physical therapist, the therapist told me, "You know, I like it when kids show that they've become comfortable enough with us that the real child comes out." Then she added with a smile, "This is the true Marie and I love it."

For the most part, Marie lived among people who accepted her and allowed her to actively negotiate shared meaning and relationships. They knew her to be anything but a "silent angel." Her assertions (in action and symbol systems) served to empower her and affirm her membership in many social contexts. She experienced few firm social borders—these seemed permeable—but some people close to Marie continued to wrestle with traditional perspectives that stigmatized her.

## EMERGING THEMES AND ASSERTIONS

Three themes emerged from constructing Marie's portrait that addressed my research questions about the nature of positive reciprocal relationships and the contexts where these develop. The most powerful theme was Marie's agency in actively engaging with others in multiple contexts. This theme was illustrated by Marie's constant calls for recognition. Her voice, in action, words, and drawings, reminded others that she was a viable member of her community with interesting stories to tell. According to Miss Grant, earlier in their relationship she and Marie "battled" one another as Marie tried to remain with her classmates in the general education classroom. She drew attention to herself by raising her hand and calling out "Look at me." Marie readily shared her opinions and preferences. She told her Grandma Aga that she preferred to talk and both her student teacher and friend Brenda that she wanted to read books. Marie actively engaged in writing, drawing, singing, book reading, and storytelling with her peers and adults. On that initial home visit, Amy said that Marie loved books, and later she observed, "Marie loves to be part of the action." Thus, Marie's agency and need to connect with others, through action, words, and drawings, served as a reminder that she had a place among her communities.

The second theme was captured by Marie's mother, who said, "You're not trying to work with a syndrome; you're trying to work with a little girl." Her comment emphasizes the importance of the other person's orientation toward Marie in how they negotiate shared meaning. The perceived role(s) of the individuals who were hired as part of Marie's support team played a large part in how Marie's forms of engagement (actions and words) were interpreted. For instance, Marie's student teacher seemed to initially approach Marie in the same way Miss Grant had: viewing her as a labeled child with a disorder who needed to be "fixed." As Miss Grant pointed out, this approach led to "battles."

Similarly, when Marie's associates viewed their role as translator, protector, and physical guide, they tended to speak on her behalf or do much of her work for her, inadvertently disempowering Marie of the speech and language she did have. By contrast, many people in Marie's social circles viewed themselves as her friend, advocate, and co-constructor of meaning. Their interpretations of Marie as a valued member and communicator reflected Kliewer and Biklen's (2007) concept of local understanding and Bogdan and Taylor's (1987/1989) sociology of acceptance. In turn, such interpretations, that involved careful listening and reflection, seemed to reduce or eliminate restrictive social borders and provide Marie with greater educational opportunities among her peers.

Marie appeared to recognize the power her facility with language and various forms of literacy afforded her in the social worlds where she lived. The fact that she expressed herself with confidence much of the time in a multitude of contexts suggests that she had learned how to make her intentions known to others and that she had taught others in her social worlds how to interpret her somewhat unconventional forms of communication. Thus, it illustrated the significance of reciprocity in positive relationships. It may also suggest that many of those "others" in her life have been willing to take what might be called "risks" of engagement, risks that are often part of any reciprocal relationships.

The third theme, overcoming perceived risks, meant that those who found meaningful ways of knowing Marie recognized her need for independence and her right to be respected. In other words, like Grandma Aga at McDonald's, they may have risked social rejection in order to honor Marie's way of communicating. Or they might have risked Marie getting hurt going down the pool slide or walking unassisted from the bus to her locker. As Miss Grant and Mrs. Perry's lesson plan meetings revealed, they needed to "back off" and let go of some of the control they may have exerted over Marie if she was to continue growing. Also, as teachers, they took professional risks by sharing power (e.g., co-teaching) and using less conventional methods of instruction (e.g., singing math) in addition to modifying for and accommodating Marie in the general curriculum.

In summary, Marie seemed drawn to use of her limited speech and other forms of expression as ways to make others aware of her presence and her rightful place among them. Despite some tensions regarding stereotypical interpretations, Marie appears to have secured her membership in her family, her school, and her community.

# CHAPTER 5

# Conclusions and Implications

Although I focused on a sociology of acceptance (Bogdan & Taylor, 1987; Taylor & Bogdan, 1989) and local understanding (Kliewer & Biklen, 2007) in the lives of three young people with significant disabilities, I found these relationships to be less than straightforward. Their stories are complex and reveal a struggle with social borders, where both communicative partners risked rejection and various forms of segregation. This echoes findings showing how paraprofessional support in K–12 and higher education settings can serve to restrict social interactions for young people with disabilities (Causton-Theoharis, Ashby, & DeClouette, 2009; Causton-Theoharis & Malmgren, 2005; Giangreco, Edelman, Luiselli, & MacFarland, 1997). The risks involved a negotiation of power sharing that, when recognized by the nondisabled partner as serving a basic human need for agency and membership, led to more positive relationship-building opportunities. The role of agency in the lives of people with disabilities is important when considering efforts to encourage self-determination practices. There seems to be a need for caregivers and support providers to relinquish aspects of their own control over particular circumstances in order to provide opportunities for people with disabilities to develop their sense of agency. This may run counter to some practices in which educators and community-based support providers have been trained to follow strict protocols that limit such opportunities. Herein lies the point of negotiation, that includes elements of risk taking, where we need to pay particular attention to the way we interact and carefully listen (and watch) those who might communicate in less than conventional ways. (For a further discussion of agency, see Sauer, 2012; Rossetti et al. 2008.)

The Hutton man's acknowledgment that they were "unaccepting of differences" seemed to accurately portray the dominant discourse of the community as a whole, but as the portraits illustrated, there were people in all three of these young people's lives who seemed to question this sentiment and who appeared willing to change what Gee

(1999) refers to as their "storylines" or "cultural models." Furthermore, all three of these young people considered to have significant disabilities showed resistance to the patterns and practices of social exclusion.

In addition to emphasizing the importance of careful listening for teachers, Cazden (2001) argues that teachers must share "speaking rights." She explains: "The most important asymmetry in the rights and obligations of teachers and students is over control of the right to speak" (p. 82). I interpret this more broadly to include students' right to express their thoughts, feelings, and opinions in any form of communication they have available to them. The international organization for the equity, opportunity, and inclusion for people with disabilities known historically as the Association for People with Severe Handicaps (TASH) adopted a Resolution on the Right to Communicate (TASH, 2000) that articulates the reasons why every effort must be made "to discover and secure an appropriate system" of communication for all people. The resolution argues that regularity and participation in inclusive contexts is a free-speech issue.

Educational contexts impact the lives not only of our students with disabilities but of all children as they become adult citizens who interact with people with disabilities in the community, at work, or in their own families and whose decisions then later influence the lived experiences of people with disabilities (Diamond & Huang, 2005; Schnorr, 1990; Siperstein, Parker, Bardon, & Widaman, 2007). The first graders in Schnorr's (1990) study answered, "Peter?" when asked about a boy who was only partly included in general education contexts, indicating they did not know him. They said, "Oh, he comes and goes", suggesting he wasn't a true member of their classroom. By contrast, Marie's classmate Brenda with whom she learned together in the general education classroom was quick to describe many details about Marie. Further, adults who work in or on behalf of educational settings, including bus drivers, cafeteria staff, and school board members, also are part of the sociocultural milieu in which young people spend a good deal of their time. As we learned through the portraits, the attitudes and resulting behaviors of these adults made a difference. This finding is similar to that of Wansart's (1995) study of teacher attitudes, showing that when teachers changed from viewing their students as having deficits to seeing then as competent learners, their students improved academically. Therefore, it is especially important to consider a holistic view when we talk about inclusive schooling.

Inclusive education is a requirement of a democratic society, as Lipsky and Gartner (2004) argued. Although the Individuals with Disabilities Education Improvement Act of 2004 focuses on the least restrictive environment for students with disabilities, studies show the value of inclusive schooling for all students (Chandler-Olcott & Kluth, 2009; Fisher, Roach, & Frey, 2000; Theoharis & Causton-Theoharis, 2010). Chandler-Olcott & Kluth (2009) suggest that students with autism who are included in general education contexts can "serve as an early warning system for pedagogical problems that are happening in the classroom as a whole" (p. 548). After having included a student with autism in their classes teachers' routines showed more varied ways in which teachers provided all students with access to literacy opportunities and changed their focus from activities to student outcomes. Fisher et al (2000) illustrate the value of moving from the discontinuity of pull-out programs to inclusive schooling as an important part of whole school reform efforts. If we are to raise a generation of students who acknowledge the ever-increasing diversity that is American, it is argued that we need to attend to the inequality and discrimination that marginalized students experience. Theoharis & Causton-Theoharis (2010) explain:

> The theory behind inclusion is that the best way to provide quality education for students with disabilities—and all students—is to increase marginalized students' access to the general education classroom, where the best curriculum and social opportunity are often provided.

The portraits of the three students described in this book illustrate the power of inclusive experience for the children, their classmates, teachers, and families.

There are an ever-growing number of research articles and texts that provide strategies supporting inclusion to which educators, counselors, therapists, principals, and others who work with students with significant disabilities can refer for guidance. Scholar and consultant Paula Kluth has written extensively about ways to support literacy for students with autism, and many of her resources are freely available on her Web site. One of my favorites is the Strengths and Strategies Profile (Kluth & Dimon-Borowski, 2003). Richard Jackson (2004), senior research scientist at the Center for Applied Special Technology (CAST) in universally designed technology and professor at Boston College, compiled a user-friendly and richly resourced report titled *Technologies Supporting Curriculum Access for Students with Disabilities* that is available on the CAST Web site along with many other current resources. There is no shortage of information about how to "do" inclusive schooling well. It is important to remind ourselves that our best teachers are our children, if we take the time to carefully listen to and watch them.

Inclusion in schools is just one social context, and ultimately, as I noted in the Introduction, we expect people with disabilities to participate in "all aspects of society" (American with Disabilities Act of 1990). One will find, for instance, "full inclusion" as one of the headings on the home page of the Office of Disability Employment Policy, which is part of the U.S. Department of Labor. Despite general improvement over the decades, the prospects for people with disabilities, particularly for those with significant disabilities, are disheartening. The Bureau of Labor Statistics (2012) reported that only 17.8 percent of persons with a disability were employed in 2011 compared with nearly 65 percent employment in the general public. The young adult population was disproportionately impacted during the recession years between 2007 and 2009, with their unemployment rates doubling. It is interesting to note that those with disabilities who were employed were more likely than their nondisabled peers to be self-employed. Self-determination during adolescence seems to play a part in the subsequent employment of people with disabilities, and "adults' perceptions may serve to limit the effectiveness of youths' efforts to self-determine" (Carter, Owens, Trainor, Sun, & Swedeen, 2009, p. 179). Therefore, it is important that we examine the communicative efforts of our youth with disabilities in order to find ways in which we might learn from them how best to support them in their efforts to participate in our society. Carter et al. (2009) noted, "Adolescence represents a particularly salient developmental period within which to promote the attitudes, behaviors, knowledge, and experiences that enhance self-determination" (pp. 179–180). In Katie's circumstances, we would certainly expect her support team to collaborate with her on exploring career options that might capitalize on her talents and interests that involved theater, music, art, and writing rather than the life skills track on which she had been previously placed.

Progress has been made, but there is much yet to be done. In 2006, for instance, the United Nations General Assembly adopted the Convention on the Rights of Persons with Disabilities, which set out a list of articles and directives for signatory countries (United Nations, 2007; see http://www.un.org/disabilities/convention/conventionfull.shtml). At the time of writing (July 2012), the U.S. Senate Foreign Relations Committee had only just approved the treaty and sent it to the full Senate for ratification, years after dozens of other so-called less developed countries. "It is never wise to assume that progress is a constant unless there is an abiding commitment to make it happen," declared Valerie Bradley in her presidential address to the members of what was then called the American Association on Mental Retardation (Bradley, 2006, p. 383). It is generally understood that in order to effect change, or to hold onto the changes for which others before us fought, we must first exercise self-awareness, and through our daily interactions, we can begin to change ourselves.

Literacy and imagination seem to act as social tools for negotiating power and relationships in families, educational settings, research, and neighborhood communities (Sauer, in press). Using a broad social definition of literacy encompassing writing, drawing, acting, reading, and music (Gallas, 2003; Kliewer, 2008), these portraits illustrate how literacy served an emancipatory prospect similar to what Giroux describes in Freire and Macedo's (1987) well-known book, *Literacy: Reading the Word and the World*, where people can "reconstitute their relationship with the wider society" (Giroux, 1987, p. 7). David was not unique as a young person who read and used visual and complicated symbolic systems of communication but who did not have reliable or discernible verbal language (Biklen, 2005; Biklen & Burke, 2006; Broderick & Kasa-Hendrickson, 2001; Crossley, 1997; Gillingham & McClennen, 2003; Kasa-Hendrickson & Broderick, 2009). Katie's proficiency with the written word and with reading words and music allowed her access to several inclusive contexts where she developed social confidence and some reciprocal relationships. David's and Marie's emerging literacies, however, were not always valued, a historical problem for people with significant disabilities (Kliewer, Biklen, & Kasa-Hendrickson, 2006). Like Katie, Marie had an interest in music. Marie's teachers sometimes put her academic work to music, and it was through music that she became the first in her religious education class to learn her prayers. Musical performances through their schools also provided Katie and Marie with greater opportunities to develop relationships with nondisabled peers. It was also in the music class where David seemed most free to move about and interact with his classmates. This interplay between the arts and literacy was important for these young people with disabilities, confirming findings in similar studies (Barton & Wolery, 2010; Gallas, 2003; Kliewer, 2008; McNair, 2008).

Although learning how to negotiate shared meaning with David, Katie, and Marie all proved to be less than straightforward, local understanding (Kliewer & Biklen, 2007) seemed to provide all three of these young people with greater opportunities for deeper, fuller reciprocal relationships to develop. Success appeared to be in part determined by the combined efforts of the young people with significant disabilities and their communication partners to resist preconceived notions of disability. Thus, local understanding where people with significant disabilities were viewed as intelligent and worthy partners in a valued relationship offered a tool for contesting the social borders that dominated the discourse patterns and habits in the greater social arena.

The concept of local understanding presumes competence (Biklen & Burke, 2006) and advocates for the least dangerous assumption (Donnellan, 1984), which turns the responsibility for shared understanding onto the person considered to be without disability. The notion of presuming competence gives the person with the disability the benefit of the doubt (Biklen & Burke, 2006; Bogdan & Taylor, 1992). "Thus, for Donnellan," suggests Jorgensen (2005),

> the least-dangerous assumption when working with students with significant disabilities is to assume that they are competent and able to learn, because to do otherwise would result in harm such as fewer educational opportunities, inferior literacy instruction, a segregated education, and fewer choices as an adult. (p. 1)

These ideas are valuable for those of us in professional preparation and training programs as well as for families and professionals in the field. Adopting these ideas necessitates critical self-reflection, such as I described in the Introduction, where I found, upon reviewing the transcripts from a recording of a family dinner conversation, that we had in fact hampered our son's communicative efforts rather than encouraged him. Despite my years of special education professional development and years teaching and providing community-based support to people with disabilities, I was inadvertently making assumptions that limited his opportunities to develop his communication proficiency. In the years since, I have had to continually step back and reflect on my own interactions, and these portraits illustrate the importance of such vigilance for all of us. If we are to embrace the calls from people with disabilities, such as "Nothing about us without us" (Charlton, 1998), we will certainly need to maintain a commitment to self-awareness as we enter into our daily interactions, particularly as we develop individual plans and make decisions that impact these individuals' lives. To begin in this effort, review the following questions and enter into discussions with your classmates or colleagues about your answers.

## GUIDING QUESTIONS FOR DISCUSSION

1. Review each of the three portraits and identify behaviors illustrating communicative intent or words spoken that illustrated the efforts of David, Katie, or Marie to assert themselves as active participants with preferences and/or opinions. Identify the circumstances that you think seemed to support their efforts.

2. Describe one scene from each of the three portraits that exemplify local understanding and discuss what you think the practitioners (or family members) said or did that enabled the reciprocal relationship to be developed.

3. In each of the three portraits, there were instances where the young people with disabilities were not acknowledged or treated as valued participants. Choose one of these instances, and using research-based resources, brainstorm alternative scenarios that could have ensued where local understanding might have developed.

4. Describe one scene from your current or future professional contexts where you (will) work with young people with significant disabilities. You may draw the scene and/or write out possible dialogue. Share your description with a partner and analyze ways in which you showed (or did not show) evidence of local understanding.

5. Describe positive examples in your profession where you could construct opportunities for young people with significant disabilities to engage in their "speaking rights." In other words, what might examples of "speaking rights" look and sound like in your professional contexts?

# References

American with Disabilities Act of 1990. 42 U.S.C. §§ 12101 *et seq.*

Amos, P. E., Donnellan, A. M., Hill, D. A., Lapos, M., Leary, M. R., Lissner-Grant, K., (2005). *Seeing movement: How our perception of movement and sensory differences can change our perception of people diagnosed with autism/PDD, mental retardation, and related disabilities.* Forest Knolls, CA: Autism National Committee.

Anzaldua, G. (1999). *Borderlands/La frontera: The new mestiza.* San Francisco, CA: Spinters/ Aunt Lute Book Company.

Ayers, W. (1989). *The good preschool teacher: Six teachers reflect on their lives.* New York, NY: Teachers College Press.

Bakhtin, M.M. (1984). *Problems of Dostoevsky's poetics* (C. Emerson & M. Holquist, Trans.). Minneapolis: University of Minnesota Press.

Barton, E. E., & Wolery, M. (2010). Training teachers to promote pretend play in young children with disabilities. *Exceptional Children, 77,* 85–106.

Becker, H. S. (1963). *Outsiders: Studies in the sociology of deviance.* New York: Free Press.

Biklen, D. (2005). *Autism and the myth of the person alone.* New York, NY: New York University Press.

Biklen, D., & Burke, J. (2006). Presuming competence. *Equity & Excellence in Education, 39,* 166–175.

Bogdan, R., & Biklen, S. K. (2003). *Qualitative research for education: An introduction to theories and methods* (4th ed.). Boston, MA: Pearson Education Group.

Bogdan, R., & Taylor, S. J. (1987). Toward a sociology of acceptance: The other side of the study of deviance. *Social Policy, 18*(2), 34–39.

Bogdan, R., & Taylor, S. J. (1992). Relationships with severely disabled people: The social construction of humanness. In P. M. Ferguson, D. L. Ferguson, & S. J. Taylor (Eds.), *Interpreting disability: A qualitative reader.* New York, NY: Teachers College Press.

Bradley, V. J. (2006). President's address 2006: Creating sustainable reform: Aligning our generational prisms. *Mental Retardation, 44,* 383–387.

Brantlinger, E., Jimenez, R., Klingner, J., & Richardson, V. (2005). Qualitative studies in special education. *Exceptional Children, 71*(2), 195–207.

Brantlinger, E. A., Klein, S. M., & Guskin, S. L. (1994). *Fighting for Darla: Challenges for family care and professional responsibility.* New York, NY: Teachers College Press.

Brantlinger, E., Jimenez, R., Klingner, J., Pugach, M. & Richardson, V. (2005). Qualitative studies in special education. *Exceptional Children, 71*(2), 195–207.

Broderick, A., & Kasa-Hendrickson, C. (2001). "Say just one word at first": The emergence of reliable speech in a student labeled with autism. *Association for Persons with Severe Handicaps, 26,* 13–24.

Broer, S. M., Doyle, M. B., & Giangreco, M. F. (2005). Perspectives of students with intellectual disabilities about their experiences with paraprofessional support. *Exceptional Children, 71*(4), 1–16.

Carter, E. W., Owens, L., Trainor, A. A., Sun, Y., & Swedeen, B. (2009). Self-determination skills and opportunities of adolescents with severe intellectual and developmental disabilities. *American Journal of Developmental Disabilities, 114,* 179–192. doi:10.1352/1944 7558 1143179

Causton-Theoharis, J., Ashby, C., & DeClouette, N. (2009). Relentless optimism: Inclusive postsecondary opportunities for students with significant disabilities. *Journal of Postsecondary Education and Disability, 22*(2), 88–105. Available at http://www.ahead.org/publications

Causton-Theoharis, J., & Malmgren, K. (2005). Increasing peer interactions for students with severe disabilities via paraprofessional training. *Teaching Exceptional Children, 71,* 431–444.

Cazden, C. B. (2001). *Classroom discourse: The language of teaching and learning* (2nd ed.). Portsmouth, NH: Heinemann.

Chandler-Olcott, K., & Kluth, P. (2009). Why everyone benefits from including students with autism in literacy classrooms. *Reading Teacher, 62,* 548–557. doi:10.1598/RT.62.7.1

Chapman, T. (2007). Interrogating classroom relationships and events: Using portraiture and critical race theory in education research. *Educational Researcher, 36*(3), 156–162. doi:10.3102/0013189X07301437

Charlton, J. (1998). *Nothing About Us Without Us.* Berkeley: University of California Press.

Connor, D. (2006, April). *Breaking containment: The power of narrative knowing—Countering silences within traditional special education research.* Paper presented at the American Educational Research Association Annual Meeting, San Francisco, CA.

Crossley, R. (1997). *Speechless: Facilitating communication for people without voices.* New York, NY: Dutton.

Crossley, R., & McDonald, A. (1984). *Annie's coming out.* Sydney: Penguin Books.

Diamond, K. E., & Huang, H.-H. (2005). Preschoolers' ideas about disabilities. *Infants & Young Children, 18*(1), 37–46.

Disney Enterprises. (2006). *High School Musical.* New York: Disney Press.

Donnellan, A. (1984). The criterion of the least dangerous assumption. *Behavioral Disorders, 9*(2), 141–150.

Donnellan, A., Leary, M., & Robledo, J. (2006). I can't get started: Stress and the roles of movement differences for individuals with the autism label. In G. Baron, J. Groden, G. Groden, & L. Lipsitt (Eds.), *Stress and coping in autism* (pp. 205–245). Oxford, England: Oxford University Press.

Ferguson, P. M., Ferguson, D. L., & Taylor, S. J. (Eds.). (1992). *Interpreting disability: A qualitative reader.* New York, NY: Teachers College Press.

Fisher, D., Roach, V., & Frey, N. (2002). Examining the general programmatic benefits of inclusive schools. *International Journal of Inclusive Education, 6*(1), 63–78.

Fraser, S., Lewis, V., Ding, S., Kellet, M., & Robinson, C. (Eds.). (2005). *Doing research with children and young people.* London: Sage.

Gallas, K. (2003). *Imagination and literacy: A teacher's search for the heart of learning.* New York, NY: Teachers College Press.

Gee, J. P. (1996). *Social linguistics and literacies: Ideology in discourses* (2nd ed.). New York, NY: Routledge Farmer.

Gee, J. P. (1999). *An introduction to discourse analysis: Theory and method.* London, England: Routledge.

Gee, J. P. (2005). *An introduction to discourse analysis: Theory and method* (2nd ed.). New York, NY: Routledge.

Geertz, C. (1983). *Local knowledge: Further essays in interpretive anthropology.* New York, NY: Basic Books.

Giangreco, M., Edleman, S., Luiselli, T., & MacFarland, S. (1997). Helping or hovering? Effects of instructional assistant proximity on students with disabilities. *Exceptional Children, 64*(1), 7–18.

Gillingham, G., & McClennen, S. (2003). *Sharing our wisdom: A collection of presentations by people within the autism spectrum.* North Plymouth, MA: Autism National Committee.

Giroux, H. (1987). Introduction. In Paulo Freire and Donald Macedo, *Literacy: Reading the word and the world.* (pp. 1–28). Westport, CT: Bergin & Garvey.

Giroux, H. (1992). *Border crossings.* London, England: Routledge.

Glaser, B. (1978). *Theoretical sensitivity: Advances in the methodology of grounded theory.* Mill Valley, CA: Sociology Press.

Goode, D. A. (1994). *A world without words: The social construction of children born deaf and blind.* Philadelphia, PA: Temple University Press.

Grandin, T., & Barron, S. (2005). *Unwritten rules of social relationships: Decoding social mysteries through the unique perspectives of autism.* Arlington, TX: Future Horizons.

Graue, M. E., & Walsh, D. J. (1998). *Studying children in contexts: Theories, methods, and ethics.* Thousand Oaks: Sage.

Holmes, R. M. (1998). *Fieldwork with children.* Thousand Oaks, CA: Sage.

Hymes, D. H. (1973). *Toward linguistic competence.* Austin: University of Texas, Department of Anthropology.

Individuals with Disabilities Education Improvement Act of 2004 (IDEA, 2004), H.R.1350, 20 U.S.C. §1400 *et seq.* Available at http://thomas.loc.gov/cgi-bin/query/z?c108:h.1350.enr:

Jackson, R. M. (2004). *Technologies supporting curriculum access to the general curriculum for students with disabilities.* Wakefield, MA: Center for Applied Special Technology.

Jorgensen, C. (2005). The least dangerous assumption: A challenge to create a new paradigm. *Disability Solutions, 6*(3), 1–15.

Kasa-Hendrickson, C. & Broderick, A. (2009). Sorting out speech: Understanding multiple methods of communication for persons with autism and other developmental disabilities. *The Journal of Developmental Processes, 4*(2), 116–133.

Kliewer, C. (2008). Joining the literacy flow: Fostering symbol and written language learning in young children with significant developmental disabilities through the four currents of literacy. *Research & Practice for Persons with Severe Disabilities, 33*(3), 103–121.

Kliewer, C., & Biklen, D. (2007). Enacting literacy: Local understanding, significant disability, and a new frame for educational opportunity. *Teachers College Record, 109*, 2579–2600.

Kliewer, C., Biklen, D., & Kasa-Hendrickson, C. (2006). Who may be literate? Disability and resistance to the cultural denial of competence. *American Educational Research Journal, 43*, 163–192.

Kluth, P. (2003). *You're going to love this kid!: Teaching children with autism in the inclusive classroom.* Baltimore, MD: Paul H. Brookes.

Kluth, P. (2004). Autism, autobiography, and adaptations. *Teaching Exceptional Children, 36*(4), 42–47.

Kluth, P., & Dimon-Borowski, M. (2003). *Strengths & Strategies Profile.* Available at http://www.paulakluth.com/readings/inclusive-schooling/strengths-and-strategies/

Kress, G. (1997). *Before writing: Rethinking the paths to literacy.* New York, NY: Routledge.

Kunhardt, D. (1962). *Pat the bunny.* Racine, WI: Golden Books.

Lawrence, D. N., & Greenberg, F. Stick to the status quo [Song]. On *High school musical.* Burbank, CA: Walt Disney Records.

Lawrence-Lightfoot, S. (1983). *The good high school: Portraits of character and culture.* New York, NY: Basic Books.

Lawrence-Lightfoot, S. (2003). *The essential cnversation: What parents and teachers can learn from each other.* New York: Random House.

Lawrence-Lightfoot, S. (2005). Reflections on portraiture: A dialogue between art and science. *Qualitative Inquiry, 11*(1), 3–15.

Lawrence-Lightfoot, S., & Davis, J. H. (1997). *The art and science of portraiture.* San Francisco, CA: Jossey-Bass.

Lewis, A., & Lindsay, G. (Eds.). (2000). *Researching children's perspectives.* Buckingham: Open University Press.

Lewis, V., & Kellet, M. (2005). Disability. In S. Fraser, V. Lewis, S. Ding, M. Kellet, & C. Robinson (Eds.), *Doing research with children and young people* (pp. 191–205). London, England: Sage.

Linneman, R. D. (2001). *Idiots: Stories about mindedness and mental retardation.* New York: Peter Lang.

Lipsky, D. K., & Gartner, A. (2004). Inclusive education: A requirement of a democratic society. In David R. Mitchell (Ed.), *Special education needs and inclusive education: Major themes* (pp. 32–44). New York, NY: Routledge Farmer.

Lloyd-Smith, M., & Tarr, J. (2000). Researching children's perspectives: A sociological dimension. In A. Lewis & G. Lindsay (Eds.), *Researching children's perspectives* (pp. 59–70). Buckingham, England: Open University Press.

Lovett, H. (1996). *Learning to listen: Positive approaches and people with difficult behavior.* Baltimore, MD: Paul H. Brookes.

MacBeath, J. (2006). Finding a voice, finding self. *Educational Review, 58,* 195–207.

Martin, B., Jr., & Carle, E. (1967). *Brown bear, brown bear, what do you see?* New York, NY: Henry Holt and Company.

Maxwell, J. A. (1992). Understanding and validity in qualitative research. *Harvard Educational Review, 62,* 279–299.

Mayer, M. (2001). *Just me and my friend.* New York: Random House.

McDermott, R. P. (1993). The acquisition of a child by a learning disability. In S. Chaiklin & J. Lave (Eds.), *Understanding practice* (pp. 269–305). New York, NY: Cambridge University Press.

McNair, S. (2008). *Current issues and evidence based practices in inclusion of children with disabilities in early childhood education: A literature review for the very special arts.* Available at http://www.vsarts.org/documents/resources/research/SWTA-LitRvw-UsingArt TeachLiteracySkills.pdf

McNeil, K. (2005). Through our eyes: The shared lived experiences of growing up attention deficit disordered. *Dissertation Abstracts International, 66*(6-A).

Paley, V. G. (2004). *A child's work: The importance of fantasy play.* Chicago, IL: University of Chicago Press.

Pugach, M. C. (2001). The stories we choose to tell: Fulfilling the promise of qualitative research for special education. *Exceptional Children, 67,* 439–453.

Rosetti, Z., Ashby, C., Arndt, K., Chadwick, M., & Kasahara, M. (2008). "I like others to not try to fix me": Agency, independence, and autism. *Intellectual and Developmental Disabilities, 46,* 364–375. doi:10.1352/2008.46:364–375

Sauer, J. (in press). The power of imagination in the lives of young people with significant disabilities. In *Youth: Responding to lives—An international handbook.* Azzopardi, A. (Ed.). Rotterdam, The Netherlands: Sense Publishers.

Sauer, J. (2012). "Look at me": Portraiture and agency. *Disability Studies Quarterly.*

Schnorr, R. F. (1990). "Peter? He comes and goes …": First graders' perspectives on a part-time mainstream student. *Association for Persons with Severe Handicaps, 15,* 231–240.

Siperstein, G. N., Parker, R. C., Bardon, J. N., & Widaman, K. F. (2007). A national study of youth attitudes toward the inclusion of students with intellectual disabilities. *Exceptional Children, 73,* 435–455.

TASH. (2000). *TASH resolution on the right to communicate.* Adopted November 1992, revised December 2000. Available at www.tash.org/dev/tashcms/ewebeditpro5/

Tassé, M. J., Schalock, R., Thompson, J. R., & Wehmeyer, M. (2005). *Guidelines for interviewing people with disabilities: Supports Intensity Scale.* Washington, DC: American Association on Mental Retardation.

Taylor, S. J. (2000). "You're not a retard, you're just wise": Disability, social identity, and family networks. *Journal of Contemporary Ethnography, 29(1),* 58–92.

Taylor, S. J., & Bogdan, R. (1989). On accepting relationships between people with mental retardation and non-disabled people: Towards an understanding of acceptance. *Disability, Handicap & Society, 4(1),* 21–36.

Theoharis, G., & Causton-Theoharis, J. (2010). Include, belong, learn. *Interventions That Work, 68(2).* Available at http://ascd.org/publications/educational-leadership.

United Nations. (2007). *Convention on the Rights of Persons with Disabilities.* New York, NY: Author.

U.S. Department of Labor. (May, 2012). *Issues in labor statistics.: Young adult employment during the recent recession.* Washington, DC: Author.

Wansart, W. L. (1995). Teaching as a way of knowing: Observing and responding to students' abilities. *Remedial and Special Education, 16(3),* 166–177.

Williams, D. (1994). *Somebody somewhere: Breaking free from the world of autism.* New York, NY: Times Books.

# Epilogue

Shortly after completing the study, I co-presented with Katie at a national advocacy conference, where she was able to use her real name. It was her first time on a plane and my first time to formally cross my own boundaries between scholarship and the personal relationships I formed with my "participants." Katie has since become an adult and she recently moved out of her parents' home into a house in the neighborhood with a friend. She continues to write and so I asked her if she wanted the last word. In response, she wrote to me about music and emotions. She wrote about her volunteer work, biking, and "ideas [like] discovering differences in other people who are your friends . . . I am different than others but they can't change what they are."

# Acknowledgements

First, I would like to acknowledge the two children and one young woman portrayed in this book along with their families who taught me the importance of paying attention. They taught me how to listen and watch more carefully. They risked many things by allowing me into their lives and for that I will be forever grateful.

I want to recognize my professors and fellow graduate students in the University of Northern Iowa's Graduate Program. In particular, I want to thank Chris Kliewer, who tirelessly and kindly mentored me during the process of becoming a scholar, a long thinker, and a clearer writer. Christi Kasa encouraged me to question everything and allowed me to find my way to deeper understanding of the various ways in which people with significant disabilities can be supported. I want to thank Amy Staples for her open-door policy and unending encouragement, who, along with Ken Bleile and Rick Traw, taught me about communication and literacy. Also, special thanks to John Smith and Deb Gallagher who introduced me to Disability Studies. I could not have completed this work without the support of my classmates, Shelly Counsell and Jodi Meyer-Mork, and especially Paula Schmidt, Debrah Fordice, and Janine Kane who shared many late nights together writing and enjoying small celebrations along the way.

Special thanks go to my colleagues at Clarke University and my bicycling buddies whose prodding and questioning motivated me to transform my dissertation into a book. But I could not have maintained the stamina I needed to complete this book without the support of my family. Throughout the fieldwork and writing, my husband Chris took on many added responsibilities and patiently listened, while my children Johann and Karl missed my bedtime stories; I am indebted to them for their understanding. I want to thank my ten siblings who carried on my parents' spirited idea that I could do anything I set my mind on.

Finally, I offer my appreciation to my editor, Lisa Marie O'Hearn, who helped see this manuscript through the process to publication.

CPSIA information can be obtained at www.ICGtesting.com
Printed in the USA
BVOW022028181212

308585BV00003B/34/P